"When I finished reading this book, I did not
artistry and politics in the service of merciful an
evidence of the inseparability of justice and beauty. The poetic
personal make it a captivating read where deep, complex learning is transformed into clarity, intimacy, and pleasure. Histories and cultural heroes are taken up here and re-examined. Art is shown as both a day-to-day reference and source of witnessing. Here, we remember that the joy of spiritual and performative writing is simultaneously and grandly enlightening. The reader enters a potpourri of spiritualities, both secular and sacred, both subaltern and soaring. The reader enters the alchemy and divinity of collaboration as a heartfelt offering toward the common good."

– **D. Soyini Madison,** *Professor Emeritus, Department of Performance Studies, Northwestern University, USA*

"Powerful and poetic, this major new work by two of the leading performance scholars in the field engages in a performative praxis of doing collaborative spirit-writing. Situated within and against the rhythms of everyday Black life in the United States, Alexander and Weems offer the act of spirit-writing as a means through which to experience, resist, and reimagine the historical present. Their rich, multi-layered, and lyrical writing emotionally grabs the reader and takes them on a journey of discovery through family histories, cultural milestones, and generational change. This is a must-read text for anyone looking to write their way into and out of our fractured – though perhaps still hopeful – social, cultural, and political futures."

– **Michael D. Giardina,** *Professor of Physical Culture and Qualitative Inquiry, Florida State University; Director, International Congress of Qualitative Inquiry, USA*

"Come to *Collaborative Spirit Writing* because you cannot fully think and feel your way through our current reckoning with U.S. structural anti-Blackness without it. Stay, and return again and again, to accompany two brilliant Black scholar-artists through an uncompromising, lyrical, and rigorously activist autoethnographic journey from 'Dedication' through 'Revolution,' 'Resistance,' and 'Reparations,' to 'Redemption.' This is critical race theory delivered in ferociously poetic and intimate dialogues: at once keenly political and deeply spiritual. You will be informed, shaken, challenged, taught, schooled, moved, and – most importantly – changed."

– **Judith Hamera,** *Professor, Lewis Center for the Arts, Princeton University, USA*

"*Collaborative Spirit-Writing and Performance in Everyday Black Lives* is a formidable conjuring of our past and present struggles, aspirations, and politics towards collective liberation. Alexander and Weems offer us a powerful dialogical performance between Black art and lived experience that meticulously navigates rather than negate difference. In doing so, they illuminate how collaborative spirit-writing and performance are potent tools to construct emergent modes of relation and relating against and beyond the Western episteme."

– **Bryce Henson,** *PhD, Assistant Professor, Department of Communication, Texas A&M University, USA*

COLLABORATIVE SPIRIT-WRITING AND PERFORMANCE IN EVERYDAY BLACK LIVES

Collaborative Spirit-Writing and Performance in Everyday Black Lives is about the interconnectedness between collaboration, spirit, and writing. It is also about a dialogic engagement that draws upon shared lived experiences, hopes, and fears of two Black people: male/female, straight/gay.

This book is structured around a series of textual performances, poems, plays, dialogues, calls and responses, and mediations that serve as claim, ground, warrant, qualifier, rebuttal, and backing in an argument about collaborative spirit-writing for social justice. Each entry provides evidence of encounters of possibility, collated between the authors, for ourselves, for readers, and society from a standpoint of individual and collective struggle. The entries in this Black performance diary are at times independent and interdependent, interspliced and interrogative, interanimating and interstitial. They build arguments about collaboration but always emanate from a place of discontent in a caste system, designed through slavery and maintained until today, that positions Black people in relation to white superiority, terror, and perpetual struggle.

With particular emphasis on the confluence of Race, Racism, Antiracism, Black Lives Matter, the Trump administration, and the Coronavirus pandemic, this book will appeal to students and scholars in Race studies, performance studies, and those who practice qualitative methods as a new way of seeking Black social justice.

Bryant Keith Alexander is a professor and Dean in the College of Communication and Fine Arts, and an Interim Dean in the School of Film and Television at Loyola Marymount University, USA. He is author or co-editor of five previous books.

Mary E. Weems is a poet, playwright, scholar, and author of 14 books including *Blackeyed: Plays and Monologues,* and five chapbooks. Weems was awarded a 2015 Cleveland Arts Prize for her full-length drama *MEAT* and has also been nominated for a Pushcart Prize. Weems may be reached at www.maryeweems.org.

Qualitative Inquiry and Social Justice

Series Editors: Norman K. Denzin and Yvonna Lincoln
University of Illinois at Urbana-Champaign and Texas A&M University

Books in this series address the role of critical qualitative research in an era that cries out for emancipatory visions that move people to struggle and resist oppression. Rooted in an ethical framework that is based on human rights and social justice, the series publishes exemplary studies that advance this transformative paradigm.

Other volumes in this series include:

Ethnotheatre
Research from Page to Stage
Johnny Saldaña

Autoethnography and the Other
Unsettling Power through Utopian Performatives
Tami Spry

Pedagogy of Solidarity
Paulo Freire, Ana Maria Araujo Freire and Walter de Oliveira

Body, Paper, Stage
Writing and Performing Autoethnography
Tami Spry

For a full list of titles in this series, please visit www.routledge.com

COLLABORATIVE SPIRIT-WRITING AND PERFORMANCE IN EVERYDAY BLACK LIVES

Bryant Keith Alexander and Mary E. Weems

NEW YORK AND LONDON

First published 2022
by Routledge
605 Third Avenue, New York, NY 10158

and by Routledge
2 Park Square, Milton Park, Abingdon, Oxon, OX14 4RN

Routledge is an imprint of the Taylor & Francis Group, an informa business

Library of Congress Cataloging-in-Publication Data
A catalog record for this title has been requested

ISBN: 978-1-032-06713-1 (hbk)
ISBN: 978-1-032-06715-5 (pbk)
ISBN: 978-1-003-20352-0 (ebk)

DOI: 10.4324/9781003203520

Typeset in Bembo
by MPS Limited, Dehradun

Like our previous book together – *Still Hanging: Using Performance Texts to Deconstruct Racism* (Brill | Sense, 2021), which can serve as a companion to *Collective Spirit-Writing* – we dedicate this project to our Black brothers and sisters, and those living in-between, who have lost their lives due to racism and bias in America.

Our collaborative spirits are with you. We stand in your place to continue the struggle to right/write wrongs and work toward a better day.

Bryant and Mary

CONTENTS

ACKNOWLEDGMENTS

We take this opportunity to sincerely thank Hannah Shakespeare, Senior Commissioning Editor, Research Methods, at Routledge, and Norman K. Denzin and Yvonna S. Lincoln, Qualitative Inquiry and Social Justice series editors for their confidence in this work, and for marshalling this project with their able and committed staff.

Special thanks to Judith Hamera, former department chair, officemate, associate dean and always friend, for our continued personal and professional relationship, and her abundant brilliance that inspires me always. To my brister, E. Patrick Johnson, whose work inspires me and many others to be fiercely quare. To my academic mentor, teacher, and colleague-friend, Dr. Elyse Lamm Pineau—I keep you with me always. And to Mary E. Weems, my collaborative spirit-writing partner, who makes it all feel so right. Thank you!

Thanks to SAGE for permission to reproduce "The Revolution *Will* Be Televised (with apologies to Gill Scott-Heron)," first appearing in the *International Review of Qualitative Research* (2021); and to the University of California Press for permission to reproduce "Dreamscapes and Escapedreams: An Autoethnography through the Art of Jerry Weems," from *Departures in Critical Qualitative Research*, 10(1), 121–138 (2021).

Special love and thanks, Patrick H. Bailey Jr., with whom I continue to develop new templates of sociality across our relationship and the society in which we live together.

Bryant Keith Alexander

Special thanks to Nathan Motta and the Dobama Theater for inviting me to be part of its "Playwrights GYM," a group of Cleveland playwrights the theater supports with regular meetings, space for staged readings and productions, and other resources. To the Ensemble Theater, the Playwrights Local Theater Company, Karamu House, and the "Dark Room" at the Cleveland Public Theater, who provided space for staged/readings of some of this work in its early stages.

I'd like to thank my husband, James Amie, for his unconditional love, patience, and unwavering support.

Mary E. Weems

1

INTRODUCTION: COLLABORATIVE SPIRIT-WRITING

Bryant Keith Alexander and Mary E. Weems

Collaborative Spirit-Writing and Performance in Everyday Black Lives is about the interconnectedness between collaboration, spirit, and writing. It is also about a dialogic engagement that draws upon shared lived experiences, hopes, and fears of two Black people: one identifying as male, one identifying as female; one identifying as *homo* and the other as *hetero*. Such terms offer social determinations, but they do not limit or vitiate the cosmologies of knowing self and other – and self as other – as companions on a journey in our joint humanity. Nor do those signifiers negate or occlude those who locate themselves in the panoply of gendered, sexed, and raced identities that make us all, always and already, both particular and plural. The *spirit* in this project is very much about a religious and nonreligious invocation: a divine essence and energy of possibility that becomes an animating principle in shifting cosmologies of faith, synergy between people, and a motivating impulse in *places and spaces* that are both *sacred and secular* – where – we all *feel the spirit* that define our beings and motivates our actions.[1]

Spirit is also a manifestation of a liberating energy of action, support, uplift, and transformation that can be considered divine as it relates to collective social activism – not unlike the spirit of the Black Lives Matter movement. Here, we can reference a practiced and embodied spirituality. We are concerned with the human spirit but not divorced from the materiality of experiencing Black bodies in a unification and activation of belief as embodied action. Each animates the other toward the possible; each draws on the verifiably real and shared ineffability of struggle that anchors each author – that anchors each other – in this project, as we find the words to articulate the struggles of living and resisting oppression. In other words, an expression of need. The project offers a collaborative framework that extends beyond the two authors and, in fact, invites the reader into an enacted commitment to social change. It recognizes that it will *take a village* to

DOI: 10.4324/9781003203520-1

transform the (spirit of the) country and world in which we live, and indeed the planet that we inhabit. Collaboration is *sine quo non* to the performance of social citizenship to which we must all claim responsibility.

Writing in this project is about the process of articulating ideas, observations, and cultural practices in words and symbols as communication and memorial. But it is also the manifestation of making internal thoughts and feelings external: a therapeutic, radical, and intentional process that has the potential to make manifest our commitments to change.[2] Writing is an activity that can have *knowledge-making* and *knowledge-transforming effects*, since it allows humans to externalize their thinking in forms that are easier to reflect on and potentially rework.[3] Writing, and the intended correlative activity of reading, can serve as *templates of sociality*. They help to render both extraordinary and everyday aspects of living "readable," and reorganize "the relationships in which these readings can occupy" to make the knowing and politics of being accessible to self – as well as to and for others.[4] In this sense, the authors also engage a practice of reflexivity. "To be reflexive is to be at once one's own self subject and direct object… subjectiviz[ing] the object, or, better, make subjectivity the human mode."[5] We write through lived experience and experienced knowing. And unlike T.S. Eliot, who wrote, "We had the experience but missed the meaning," we – Bryant and Mary – understood the meaning of racism when we experience it. We now seek to re-approach experience and revisit meaning, "to restore the experience in a different form" so others can see it.[6] And we invite the reader into that practice, possibility, and potentiality.

So, in this project we are not seeking to teach a methodological process of *collaborative spirit writing* as much as engage in a performative praxis of *doing it*. This is linked with the intention of identifying and noting aspects of struggle in everyday living (in Black life), to which writing and reading could provide insight and motivation to change. The project offers "subtle [and not so subtle] tactics of resistance and private practices that make everyday living a subversive art" and promote *subversive art as practices of everyday living*.[7] Also, in the spirit of James Baldwin and so many of our Black poets and novelists, we write "in order to change the world, knowing perfectly well that [we] probably can't, but also knowing that literature is indispensable to the world. […] The world changes according to the way people see it, and if you alter even but a millimeter the way people look at reality, then you can change it."[8] We seek to change the world anyway.

In this sense, as two individuals of African-American descent who are identified as Black in America, the project also brings into confluence spirit, soul, and social justice as defining hallmarks of intention and interanimating commitments of focus. And while *soul* can be linked with a religious essence of the person that transcends death – or rather, ascends to heaven from the body after death – we are interested in the link between soul and passion made manifest through *African-American expressive culture*.[9] Through a cultural poetics of daily life experience, movements of the spirit are embodied, expressed, and publicly relayed, such that they transmit the yearning of the spirit and the *souls of Black folks*.[10] Noting the sentiment from the *Queen of Soul*, Aretha Franklin, "Soul is Black." And by extension, "Soul is the stuff of our dreams and marks the magical domain of powerful nothingness where fantasies and ancestors live." Through soul, Black folks manifest our *Black power, politics, and pleasure.*[11]

The bonds of spirit, soul, and social justice "have been treated without respect, as though they were irrelevant for analytical purposes."[12] Focusing on individuality and a degree of objectivity that privileges being disconnected from emotion as something to strive for. (Here, we're reminded of how often we witness white folks apologize for crying.) This orientation helps the powerful remain in power by limiting the possibility of our ever coming together as one nation under the God millions of us profess to believe in. For us, the features of humanness link belief, passion, and action toward articulating desire – desire as both embodied and aspirational for self and society. To be *spirit strong*[13] is to claim the fullness of one's essence and identity against social derision; to be *soulful* is to lead with the articulation of one's deep *spiritual strivings* and *spiritual yearnings*;[14] and to work for *social justice* is to make right the promise of our collective humanity, and for Black folks to celebrate and make right the sacrifices of our ancestors.[15] We strongly believe that *spirit-writing is what Black folks do* as a critical act of reconvening, recovering, and always remembering the past in relation to what is and what is yet to come. Like the ancient Negro spirituals with roots in our enslavement, Black people live within the bond of spirit, soul, and the yearning for social justice as daily practice.

Collaborative Spirit-Writing and Performance in Everyday Black Lives is structured around a series of textual performances, poems, plays, dialogues, calls-'n'-responses, and meditations that serve as claim, ground, warrant, qualifier, rebuttal, and backing in an argument about collaborative *spirit* writing in, as, and for social justice.[16] Each entry evidences encounters of possibility, collated between the authors, with and for ourselves, the readers, and society – all from a standpoint of individual and collective struggle.

Such encounters always have a beginning with the finger on the pulse *on the pulse* of the possible. Here, was our beginning: of the possible. Here, was our beginning: "*Taking the Pulse*: Looking for the Poetic and Performative in Terrorism and Hate."[17]

BRYANT: Working with Mary is like entering a space of possibility where thoughts and words comingle to tease the imagination, but then make manifest what the heart yearns to speak and the soul longs to hear. *A collaborative spirit-writing* emerges from the depths of shared racial/cultural experiences that teeters between the happy-sad/angry-joyfulness of everyday life, and the celebration-mourning/ remembrance-remorsefulness that make us human. These experiences each co-inform to, in, and of the other.

MARY: The first time I saw Bryant, we were at the International Congress of Qualitative Inquiry (ICQI) and part of a Plenary session which included Peter

McLaren. Once the session was over, I remember watching him prepare to leave and wanting to introduce myself, but I didn't. I recall that now as I read his description of our work as *collaborative spirit-writing*, because I've always had the feeling that we're connected by blood. One of the results of the diaspora of slavery is that those of us who were dragged here have been scattered through sale and/or escape throughout this country, making it difficult – if not impossible – to know who belongs to who. As Black people from different genders, generations, sexual orientations, and religious/non-religious backgrounds, we still find connections and disconnections through our upbringing, our commitment to using our work to speak out against social injustice, and for the kind of empathy, respect, and love possible when we share openly and honestly from our experiences, learning from and with each other.

BRYANT: Yes, working collectively with Mary is in part bridging the diasporic disbursal of our shared origins with lived experience mediated by time and distance. We find a recognition of the self in our co-writing, our co-presencing, our co-performing – each embodied and voiced – and in our recognition of the self in/as the other. It is that dialectical performativity of Black people that is so familiar no matter where you travel. It's as if you have met before, even though you haven't, *but of course you have* – because recognition, like memory, is more than just skin deep. It is soul deep.

Mary looks and sounds like my people, with the features of a shared nation-state. Writing with her becomes a kind of family reunion. You know, those family reunions where you are happy to see and engage people who sprang from intersecting blood lines; people with *bodies that most often look like yours* in which you begin to narrate genealogies like *theories of the flesh*. These are meetings where "the physical realities of our lives – our skin color, the land or concrete we grew up on, our sexual longings – all fuse to create a politic born of necessity. Here, we attempt to bridge the contradictions in our experience. [...] We do this bridging by naming ourselves and by telling our stories in our own words."[18]

In such reunions, these are theories of affection when you encounter knowledge of yourself that is foreign, and sometimes of its opposite when you witness some parts of yourself that are all too familiar.[19] Such reunions can not only be fun, but they also entail relational work. This work is a labored endeavor of collaborative effort – a striving toward mutually satisfying outcomes. It is a gesture "to perform as an intended and desired task." Maybe, it is work in the sense of negotiating common experiences, perceptions, or politics. And maybe it is work, such as in this collaborative project, as an act of recuperation, reconciliation, and reunification. The particularity of this co-editing team is also evidence of the need to build strong alliances between gay/straight, homo/hetero, and otherwise politically queer allies against the forces of terrorism and hate. Collectively working on/as the disarticulations and disentanglements of how we have been racialized, gendered, sexed, and alienated. We move toward an intentional enjambment of experiences, words, and worlds in which *the meaning of our lives runs over, spills over from words and actions like poetry – from one poetic line to the next, without punctual termination.*[20] A reunion, in this case, is a seamless interplay of souls and lived experiences acquainting each to the other.

MARY: Working together on the Special Issue [of *Qualitative Inquiry*, in 2016][21] was a collaborative spirit-writing, a "reunion," our ideas shared and embraced like dance partners taking turns leading without missing a step. We agreed on most of the papers, and when I was moved to respond to Dustin Bradley Goltz's "The NonSense,"[22] Bryant responded to my response constructing connections between Goltz, and my response to Goltz in the following poem:

Bryant

dancing a different dance
dancing to a dirge
dancing dodging bullets
with other colored bodies
dipping and turning
swaying and kicking without joy
a frenetic escape

Mary

music continues
gunfire pops
like bursting light bulbs,
a different rhythm
a different dance
dance of derision
dance of self-hate
choreographed on other bodies
dancing to a different rhythm

Bryant

danced a dance of religion turned mean
he danced a dance of self-hatred turned outward
a dance that Trumps volition

Both

one to three,
one two three,
one two three,

Mary

The music has stopped
I am a state of silence.
bodies are still dancing.
dancing the dance of history
of hatred
of difference
of raced/sexed/gendered bodies
of Stonewall
of Black churches.

Both

A Trans woman is stabbed by the vigil
Bleeding on top of it all

Bryant

Black boys who looked at White women
are swinging
are shuffling
tar and feathered dances
gunfire pops
like bursting light bulbs.
dancing history and culture.
Bodies leaning into
Sensedance
Dancingsense

Mary

dancing with a purpose
samba and stomping
bolero and buck-and-wing
carico and cha-cha

Bryant

Conga and chaconne
farruca and flamenco
mambo and matachin
the soul train [*Say it like Don Cornelius!*]
one two three, kick ball chain
one two three, kick ball chain

one two three, kick ball chain
all the way to 50

Both

Dancing Communities[23]
dancing as celebration and survival
dancing as freedom
dancing as "civic culture"
dancing as being
a map of something
a how to breathe
way to see real
and radical

Mary

What the hell do I do with that?

Both

Dance.[24]

[*The last word "Dance" is delivered to each other. THE PERFORMERS then exit the stage without pause and return to their seats. This is the end of the ICQI panel performance. What follows is the continuation of dialogue on the collaborative process in constructing the essay for the Special Issue.*]

BRYANT: During our collaboration, Mary introduced me to the construct of "a found poem," the responsive technique that gave rise to the previous poetic response. In our exchanges, she described the found poem "as one way of more deeply engaging a text, of interweaving your feelings/ thoughts with the original author by pulling lines that draw you in like lifelines, making you spend time, to think, to pause, to call and respond." The result is a dialogic response that stands alone and in relation to the inspiring poem.[25]

In many ways, that approach might have also characterized our entire collaboration. It offers an example of a critically shared poetic responsiveness to the work submitted in which we established an intersubjective communion as co-editors, authors, readers, listeners, and respondents – all to the submitted work – in relation to projected intent of the Special Issue. As Mary wrote earlier, we agreed on most of the accepted submissions. But in a Special Issue that called for "poetic and performative responses," the terms sometime needed negotiation.

Do the terms poetic and performative speak to form, or do they serve as a function of doing?[26] In the Special Issue, there are clear entries that are written as poetry, appearing and exhibiting a drama of verse, meter, and rhyme, with a rhythmicity of lyricism that invokes the poetic imagination – and a depth of projected meaning with an economy of words. Other selections had a narrative structure with storytelling that was no less poetic in ways that were *evocative, metonymic, subjective, nervous, citational*, and *consequential* as qualities of performative writing.[27] Each enacts a *poiesis* of making, and a *kinesis* of doing; each invites the reader into the world of the text through the author's aesthetic articulation of seeing, knowing, and experience. The variation of the two suggestive stylistics did not require compromise. It required each of us to orient ourselves to the notion of poetic and performative responses as co-informing intentions and effects of *writing as performance* and *performance as writing*.[28]

MARY: I agree with Bryant. Our Special Issue collaboration could be described as a found poem, a reciprocal word-parlance, the kind of spirit-work that happens when two people go with the flow created by an ancestral kinship coupled with working toward a common goal, each being open to the other's interpretations, suggestions, and ideas. While I write across genres, first and foremost I'm a poet, and the concise, figurative use of language permeates everything I create. My role as a poet and artistic-scholar who uses writing as both my research tool and method is to speak truth to power. When traumatic, unjust, insane acts, like the Pulse Night Club, tragedy happen in Orlando and all over this country *ad nauseum*, my first response is a poem. I've often attempted to maintain a journal, but inevitably what begins as prose shapeshifts into poetry.

During our collaboration, Bryant helped me see the "performative" aspects of submissions I'd read as straight, literal prose – lacking the imagery, simile, metaphor, rhyme, and rhythm of poetry – still told an important story. One of Bryant's many editorial strengths is his ability to read a draft and see what's not there, taking the author's central thesis and main points and articulating how the work could be re-ordered and expanded in places, resulting in a more succinct, cohesive piece. In terms of the role of the language arts in sociopolitical protest, there has never been a social movement that did not include the creative use of language as a political act. We are a nation founded on and governed by words, and the Trump presidency and its message of hate against Blacks, Jews, Muslims, the LGBTQ+ community, and immigrants places a crucial emphasis on the importance of writing, speaking, and peacefully raging against hate, and for justice, respect, and peace.

BRYANT: Mary's preceding words are a painful reminder to me. Because I am only finding my way back to poetry after years of being beaten into submission of "scholarly writing." A political edict in graduate school disciplined my psyche as it attempted to discipline my writing, even at a time when the efficacy of the performative turn had already been established. But perhaps disciplining the scholar is less an invalidation of the poetic and performative, and maybe more so an invalidation of the ritual violence involved in *rites of passage* in graduate programs. I found my way through and back to the poetic and performative – for this voice does all, and more – through the spirit of my thinking and feeling body.

Mary helped me to better see the critical in the poetic submissions I read as wordplay. What I'd read as perceptually lacking at times in the depth of evidence in fact used a different form of citation by telling the story through the felt sensation of experience; it represented a different kind of argument building, a rhythmicity of engagement that both danced and moved me. One of Mary's many editorial strengths is her ability to read poetry and find not just the imagery, simile, metaphor, rhyme, and rhythm, but to identify how meaning flows through that structure. She offers the author, and a coeditor, gentle ways of seeing how to tweak and maybe twerk – a poetic turn to dynamize the intended impact of the messaging. Thus, she is always invoking the literal and imaginative aspects of what poetry does to help us think and feel into the world of the text, and the worlds which those texts critique. The choreography of our editorial dance was poetic and performative.

In responding to this process, the process of collaboration, I have been writing in a liminal space. I write in an imagined space before Orlando and since Orlando. writing and contemplating this essay in the anniversary-time of the Orlando massacre and my birthday, June 12. The synchronicity of the two originally spawned the idea of the Special Issue.

I am
still living,
still mourning,
still writing,
still dancing;
as an act of resistance.

MARY: The linguistic beatdown Bryant references was a major concern my first semester as a doctoral student. It's in part what led to the question which informed my dissertation: When I write in scholarship mode, do I stop being a poet? I responded no:

The homogeneity of the…blah, blah, blah and Scooby Doo –
Long strings of 25-dollar words
dense as swamp mud

move from eye to surface of brain
tossing them out one-by-one.
For hours on end
bent elbow
pen hovers
head bangs on reading
wake up! Coffee
re-read
Sleeeeeeeeeep.................
Today I am – still.

BRYANT: I am also – still.

That stillness does not come from completely resisting one over the other, from but finding a place in-between: an interpenetration of each to and with the other.[29] This is where I live both in my personal and academic life: between. Such a space is not liminal, but a fixed location of possibility tethered to potentiality. It allows me to be positioned in such a way to ask some of the critical questions that guided this Special Issue (and now this book). And then we read and write those possibilities in two-voices that are neither competitive nor compensatory. For example:

How do we find the poetic and performative in terrorism and hate? The question was not directed to the actuality of terrorism and hate. For while each invokes a performative act of doing, there is nothing poetic in acts of violence that implicate the horrifics of humanity. There is nothing beautiful and poignant in the *use of intentionally indiscriminate violence as a means to create terror among masses of people; or fear to achieve a financial, political, religious, or ideological aim.*[30] This describes not only what happened in Orlando, Las Vegas, and Charlottesville, but in other national and international contexts and locations that we ritually mourn and commemorate, like war. As we also resist and endure histories of racism, sexism, homophobia, violence against people of color – and, in the Trump administration, traumatized immigrants along the Mexican borders – such acts should force us all to question our independence. They are situations in which a "powerful will bending [and a] blind persistence with which men and women believe they have a right to impose a private will upon a fellow creature."[31]

Mary and I were really interested in the poetic and performative response to terrorism and hatred. How do we respond to such a brutal tragedy? How do we make sense of the senseless? How do we grieve the loss of so many? How do we protest the changing tides of our historical present?[32] How do people use poetry and performative writing to deal with pain or loss; a truly poetic justice, if you will? How can the politics and beauty of words serve as the immediate tools to penetrate and heal a wounded soul, offering an outlet to pain, solace to suffering, a rhetorical and artistic rage of resistance? How can they build a "mobilizing praxis, breaking the discursive limits of the emperor's stages, and invigorat[e] the dynamics of democratic contest in which the emperor and his new clothes (or lack thereof) are not continually refigured"?[33]

I believe that we determined each piece included in the Special Issue gave voice to singular and collective trauma;

a direct response *to*,
a witnessing *of*,
a personalizing *in*,
a calling *out*,
a locationing *at* the site of trauma, along with
a tracing of unsettled and contested impulses
a joining and conjoining,
a spiritual activism and soul healing in the war years,
a recall/remembrance/remorse,
*a pulse/pulsing/*pulsating response,
a listening to brown queer bodies
a taking of the pulse: from death to resurrection and back
a grieving – after, (an)other
a dancing, birth/ing, after birth, second birth – reaching.[34]

As Judith Hamera writes in the Special Issue: "It posits the reach – the moment when outstretched arms move toward, for, and sometimes with another – as the kinesthetic unit incarnating dance's political-affective potential." It was this, that, these, and those gestures in the Special Issue that spoke not only to dance, and the occasion of terrorism while dancing, but further signaled how poetic and performative responses "create communities of shared labor across difference in troubled times."[35] The pieces that were not chosen did the work differently, neither less poetic nor less performative; they were simply "different dances" in relation to the choreography of the Special Issue. There is no doubt that each of those submissions will find its rightful home and do its intended work: critique and commemorate the "calamities and absurdities" of the Orlando massacre, and "the adult world" in which bodies and tensions rub against each other in ways that are not always pleasurable.[36]

MARY: Bryant's reference resonates with my life before beginning the Ph.D. journey. For years, I tried to find space "in-between," to successfully maneuver between the White, corporate world I worked in for 18 years, and my personal life as a socially conscious Black/woman living in a racist, sexist, hetero, and homophobic society. But my spirit was dying.

I finally figured out who I'm still becoming and what I'm supposed to be doing. I belong on the margins. The space of living and responding always from the cultural lens of a Black/woman from a poor, working class background, embracing where she's from and using it as a foundation for being, while learning to empathize across race, ethnicity, class, culture, gender, and sexuality with love and understanding. This positionality is why I was drawn to Goltz's piece "Non-Sense," including when he writes about a post-Pulse tragedy office visit by one of his students:

> "He is queer. He is a man of color standing almost 7 feet tall. He is the first person anyone sees in a room. He feels like a target. He's asking me if he should go to Pride this weekend, if his nearly 7-foot black body is safe, and fuck fuck fuck fuck, no."[37]

Like Goltz's student, I feel like a target. I often feel unsafe, yet I struggle to live proud and out loud – refuse to be silent in the aftermath of hatred and violence. Collaborating with Bryant and others working in and outside the academy is part of my lifeline. The articles in our Special Issue provide hope in a so-called "post-truth" "Un-tied" States, where everything shared through social media must be critically examined and fact checked. In a country where Nazis, racists, rapists, sexists, and homo- and trans-phobes are welcomed and encouraged by the president to act – to kill.

Now more than ever, we need to dance: put on our favorite shoes and let our words and bodies dance all over Trump's fucked-up plans for our country. Reach out for new partners, develop new spaces of protest, struggling forever against all forms of terror, responding to hate with everything but.

Dancing Together: A Conclusion (or a was it a Beginning?)

Working together was a "collaborative spirit-writing" – not just as cooperation in an engaged activity, but as *collaborative spirits* as *incorporeal but ubiquitous, non-quantifiable* co-presences of a shared humanity.[38] Both with hauntings from our pasts, and materialized embodiments of our current realities. Each conjured from a co-informing heritage of oppression, *feeling like a target* and *feeling unsafe*, yet finding strength in a kindled kindredness.

We previously described ourselves as "Black people from different genders, generations, and sexual orientations." That description marks both palpable differences and divisions that are not entirely distinct, given the immeasurability of identity politics and borders like desire and flesh that bleed. Those of us living in the margins must learn to thrive. The description also invokes a communion with the ineffable tensiveness that makes collaboration possible: a holding of each in relation to the other with a common commitment to the importance of doing, being, and living with pride – and out loud. It represents the ability to find, as Mary wrote, "connections/disconnections through our upbringing, our commitment to using our work to speak out against social injustice and for the kind of empathy, respect, and love possible when we share openly and honestly from our experiences, learning from and with each other."

Through the *collaborative spirit* as defined comes the *writing*: a relational *medium of human communication that represents language and emotion with signs and symbols.*[39] Sometimes writing is poetic and performative, sometimes scholarly but always dialogic; it is always invitational, and always imbued with time, place, practice, voice, style, and history. Each pivots on structures of cultural knowing that inform the articulation of experience: same and not the same, co-informing for a diverse community of readers and writers, as the contributors to this Special Issue evidence. *Collaborative Spirit-Writing* as an emerging poetic and performative methodology which we will continue to define further in word and deed.

For these and other reasons that are felt but not stated, this collaboration was easy. It sets the stage for future possibilities;

> a publication,
> a performance,
> a play,
> a finger *on the pulse* of what's next.[40]
> Always remembering
> what has already happened;
> histories that we must not forget,
> and stories that we must consistently and collectively tell.

★★★★★★★★★★

Such encounters of possibility continue to define our collaborative engagement and the outcomes we produce, like this book project. They draw the spirit from informing and competing aspects of our personal, professional and academic lives, and make those experiences manifest in a progressive, performative politics of action.

BRYANT: For the last 15 years, up until the very moment of this writing, I have worked in administrative environments that have heralded "collaboration" as a hallmark of the mediated human social engagement in doing the work of higher education administration. Said hallmark has been poked, prodded, promoted, and at time punished in pursuit of working across borders and boundaries of disciplines for the perceived "greater good" – of the institution and for those who we serve.[41] The spirit of collaboration to which I speak is expressed in the shifting nomenclature of the time. These include: breaking down silos, shared governance, and recently, the return of "interdisciplinarity" as a mantra that bleeds cosmological borders. What follows is an attempt to enrich creative ways of thinking and transforming, or of meeting the world's greatest needs by drawing from the best minds and

> thinkers across disciplinary boundaries, from different schools of thought, in order to inform a holism of information, formation, and transformation of self and society.

I embrace the ideals that undergird such thinking. Yet, the spirit of such collaborative invention is often interrupted, exercised, or even exorcised by the competitive demands that always underly educational processes. Whether it is the competition that exists between students, teachers, or departments, or that which exists in the form of rewards given for innovation, these conflicts further motivate knowledge produced in isolation and promote productivity as hallmark of creativity, instead of championing the deeply immersive possibilities of what emerges in the struggled places in between. The regional and national rankings systems further use comparisons and competitiveness to define institutional value.

These programs are all important in consideration of the funding and fundraising that sustain enrollment, revenues, and the viability of educational markets. Hence, the beginning of the push for collaboration does originate in spaces of possibilities, but it devolves into something that does not always look or feel like community.

> **Collaboration** (as in a joint participation toward a synergized goal) → **Comparison** (creating of hierarchies of value, not relational truths, with issues of "who gets credit") → **Critical** (as in finding fault, not discovering truth) → **Competition** (as in pitting *colleagues* against each other, in a failed *collegiality*) → **Compensatory** (as in a literal or figurative cost to be paid for social damage) ≠ which is not equal to striving toward **Consensus** (building agreed on standards of *cooperation* and *conciliation*) ≠ which is not **Contributory** to the building of **Collegiality** ≠ which is not equal to **Community** and the struggles toward the ***collective*** uplift that is at the core of social justice.

In describing this phenomenon, I am not demonizing my colleagues at the multiple universities where I have served in administrative roles. Surely in my own Meyers Briggs assessment, I find myself in that tensive location between *competition* and *harmony*: always trying to lean into harmony but recognizing the potentials of healthy and necessary competition as stimulus for innovation.[42]

I am using this description in administrative contexts to signal the liberatory ways in which Mary E. Weems and I are seeking to embody and exemplify a collaborative spirit-writing that is very much informed by administrative processes of knowledge production and informed action. Spirit-writing is about bleeding the borders between cosmologies of knowing ourselves in the world – which we both embrace and resist – and how we work with each other in the ebbs and flows of social activism through performance and performative texts linked to the struggles in the everyday real. The "real" is a recognition of those factors in everyday living that impact not only our mobility in place and space, but how we seek to "turn private troubles into public issues" in a collaborative negotiation of form, structure, and voice – the critical tools of liberation from our own Black and gendered oppressions in America.[43] These are also informed and undergirded by Dr. Martin Luther King Jr.'s four steps to a nonviolent civil rights campaign. These are first:, *identifying and proving the existence of injustices*; peaceful *negotiation* for change; and *self-purification* as an act of critical self-reflection on our own moral strength, to withstand the violence inflicted upon us without retaliating in ways that perpetuate the injustices we seek to transform, with our own clean hands, in the fight for justice. This process is followed by an engaged, nonviolent direct *action* that fosters the need for negotiation amongst an identified group previously nonresponsive to negotiation or change.

Always reaching for freedom.

Collaborative Spirit-Writing, the book, stands as part of a broader project of nonviolent activism and liberation through performance and performative texts. It recognizes that in each movement of the project, there are tensions in which people and actions, histories and practices, are called into question – and are *called out* and questioned. And following the cue of Martin Luther King Jr., writing in his *Letter from the Birmingham Jail,* we recognize that tension is what expands minds, challenges past traditions, and instills the possibility of critical societal change. It is the tension, the uncomfortable feeling that calls people out, that creates the potential for engagement and attending to our joint complicity – and potentially moves us all toward a more collaborative commitment to a social change. It is the foundation of a social change that builds community through diversity, equity, and inclusion. Dr. King wrote that, "True peace is not merely the absence of tension; it is the presence of justice." We extend this prophetic logic to state that true justice is not just momentary reparations for historical harms; it is reparations-plus, or a systemic shift in policies, practices, procedures, and psyches for knowing the self in relation to the other. It is a longitudinal commitment to – and promotion of – diversity, equity, inclusion and the empowered dignity of all life through the traditions of *information, formation, and transformation* of self and society.[44] And while justice is a thing achieved through action, it is also a force held in a *tensive* relation between the past, present, and future – a relational dynamic that needs to consistently exist as a commitment to maintain and sustain the equity of human social relations, through and over time, in what we call culture.

Qualitative research methods that examine and comment on culture through writing about lived, embodied, and observed behaviors are bonded in this belief and in this practice. They recognize, once again, that tension is critical in unearthing the comforts and discomforts of the status quo, with the shared and committed relief of justice. We realize that justice is maintained through an ongoing recognition of the *tensiveness,* a force-filled relationality that holds us all yoked between the past, present, and future. Our ongoing commitments to living in the realm of the possible are anchored in remembrance, leaning toward futures of potentiality, as an ongoing process for which we continually strive for social justice – always as *a thing doing* and not *a thing done.*[45] The selections in this project live to both agitate the tensions in everyday living, and to seek to recognize the importance of maintaining the tensiveness between remembrance and remorse for progressive purposes in the future.

Such encounters of possibility are always comparable to what currently exists as liberatory practices of collaboration, and not as competitive approaches to social meaning-making.

BRYANT: This current project is not about building theories of performance *or* writing, nor does it seek to build another qualitative methodology – though it does contribute, as we have in our previous work, to practices of critical and analytical human social engagement, such as *collaborative autoethnography* as "a qualitative research method that is simultaneously collaborative, autobiography, and ethnographic."[46] Our approach engages a collaborative and co-informing effort between two or more people reflecting on what appears as a common phenomenon or experience of engagement. Investigated and reflected upon from the individual perspectives, the collaborative encounter reveals an assemblage of – and diversity within – individuals. It is a collaborative comparative of experience that illuminates co-cultural knowing in-between and beyond.[47]

Collaborative Spirit-Writing works in parallel purpose to the important work of *feminist scholarship* that, in short, is a writing and theorizing through women's issues and challenges – particularly those originating from oppressive, exclusionary, and discriminatory practices built into the very cultural structures of our society. This work brings to research the "self-consciously political values of the women's movement and challenges [to] traditional notions about research," while challenging the notion of gender not as fixed but – like so many other constructions, including race and sexuality – socially constructed.[48] *Collaborative Spirit-Writing* also works in tandem with *feminist pedagogies* that are grounded in a feminist ideology that seeks to reorient the processes of teaching, upending the relational dynamics between teachers and students to reimagine the classroom as a space of possibility where hierarchies of authority between teachers and students are dismantled. Thus accomplished, a co-informing exchange of possibility is created. This cluster of conceptual frames and practices sees teachers and students in a collective and collaborative co-presence within the whole educational endeavor. They exist as learning resources to and for one another, thus transforming all participants and enabling them to transcended the knowledge they acquire in the reimagining possibilities of being and knowing. The result is a series of co-informing processes and potentials in living for self and society – processes and potentials that recognize and value the critical role that individual culture and the ideologies of both teachers and students play in educational reform and transformation.[49]

Collaborative spirit-writing also draws upon the emancipatory and equalizing potential of *invitational rhetoric* as a means of redefining rhetoric away from persuasion, manipulation, and the effort to change others. Rather, it becomes a means for establishing a relationship between interested parties engated in a communicative act that is rooted in equality, immanent value, and self-determination toward mutual transformative ends and possibilities.[50] Along with antecedents in nonviolent/collaborative communication, collaborative spirit-writing is grounded in the assumption that all human beings have capacity for compassion and empathy, and that people only resort to violence or behavior harmfully toward others when they do not know or recognize more effective strategies for meeting their needs.[51] The collaborative spirit-writing practice is inspired by our own approach of using nonviolent communication to combat the violence of everyday.

Collaborative Spirit-Writing is a project that builds performance as political praxis – an articulation of embodied doing that bridges theory and practice as evidence of knowing and a call to action. Each of the texts within this project have been written for performance. They have been performed for diverse audiences, and are slated to be performed for political purposes: to make real the rage of our engagement; to make palpable the possibilities of performance to penetrate the sensibility of self and the other as political activity; to enact theory through an embodiment of doing. Each piece was written within a time frame of our collective spirit searching, with the writing that emerged providing evidence of process. In times of Covid-19, during a contested and contestable United States presidential election and transition, and throughout the important activism of the Black Lives Matter movements, we found a dialogical partnership in the sense-making of our collaborative spirit-writing.

The entries in this Black performance diary are at times independent and interdependent, interspliced and interrogative, interanimating and interstitial. They build arguments about collaboration, while always emanating from *the origins of our discontent* in a caste system, designed through slavery and maintained until today, that positions Black people at the lowest possible status to maintain white superiority in a hierarchy of terror and perpetual struggle.[52] Each entry is grounded in the very spirit of human social encounter as necessity for surviving and thriving in our particularity and plurality, whether in academia or as independent scholar, with each of us working toward social justice and unified in purpose as Black people living in America. Such engaged qualities also move toward building arguments about a collaborative spirit-process of sense making that transcends the products of each piece and speaks to a broader ethic of critical and performative reflection that dynamizes the possibilities of being and becoming. We invite you to join us in *Collaborative Spirit-Writing and Performance in Everyday Black Lives*.

Notes

1 See Johnson, E.P. (1998). Feeling the spirit in the dark: Expanding notions of the sacred in the African-American gay community. *Callaloo, 21*(2), 399–416. http://www.jstor.org/stable/3299441
2 Bryant currently serves as a Dean, College of Communication and Fine Arts at Loyola Marymount University in Los Angeles. One of the departments in the college has a graduate program in Marital and Family Therapy with a specialization in art therapy. For him, this is one of the goals and techniques of clinical art therapy: using creative artistic expression – and the meaning-making symbols of art – to make internal thoughts and feelings external as a therapeutic process of self-discovery and recovery.
3 Estrem, H. (2015). Writing is a knowledge-making activity. In L. Adler-Kassner & E. Wardle (Eds.), *Naming what we know: Threshold concepts of writing studies* (pp. 55–56). Utah State University Press.
4 Hamera, J. (2007). *Dancing communities: Performance, difference and connection in the global city* (p. 23). Palgrave Macmillan.
5 Turner, V. (1983). A review of 'Ethnopoetics'. In Jerone Rothenr berg & Diane Rothenberg (Eds.), *Symposium of the whole: A range of discourse toward and ethnopoetics* (p. 338). University of California Press.
6 Eliot, T.S. (1944). The Dry Savages. Part 2. In *Four Quartets*. London: The Folio Society.
7 DeCerteau, M., Giard, L., & Mayol, P. (1998). *The practice of everyday life: Living and Cooking. Vol. 2.* University of Minnesota Press.
8 Romano, J. (1979, Sept. 23). James Baldwin writing and talking. *The New York Times.* https://www.nytimes.com/1979/09/23/archives/james-baldwin-writing-and-talking-baldwin-baldwin-authors-query.html. This quote is cited and drawn from my brothers Marcelo Diversi and Claudio Moreira in their important work (2018). *Betweener Autoethnographies: A Path Towards Social Justice.* Routledge. It is further cited in Diversi, M., Gale, K., Claudio, M., & Wyatt, J. (2020, December 2020). Writing with: Collaborative writing as hope and resistance. *International Review of Qualitative Research.* https://doi.org/10.1177/1940844720978761.
9 White, S., & White, G. (1998). *Stylin': African American expressive culture from its beginnings to the zoot suit.* Cornell University Press.
10 DuBois, W.E.B. (1989). *The souls of black folk.* Penguin Books.
11 Guillory, M., & Green, R.C. (Eds.). (1998). *Soul: Black power, politics, and pleasure* (p. 1). New York University Press.
12 Here Victor Turner (1979) is talking about "the deep bonds between body and mentality, unconscious and conscious thinking, species and self," 93. [Dramatistic Ritual/Ritual Drama: Performative and Reflexive Anthropology," The Kenyon Review, 1.3: 80-93.]
13 Wallace-Sanders, K. (Ed.). (2002). *Skin deep, spirit strong: The black female body in American culture.* The University of Michigan Press.
14 See the inspiring text "Of Ours Spiritual Strivings" in DuBois, W.E.B. (1989). *The souls of black folk* (pp. 3–12). Penguin Books. See also Dillard. C.B. (2007). *On spiritual strivings: Transforming an African American woman's academic life.* SUNY series in Women in Education; Barnes, C.M. (1991). *Yearning: Living between how it is how it ought to be.* Intervarsity Press; Spitzer, R.J. (2015). *The soul's upward yearning: Clues to our transcendent nature from experience and reason.* Ignatius Press.
15 For a brief bibliography on social justice, see: Adams, M., & Blumenfeld, W. (2013). *Readings for diversity and social justice* (third edition). Routledge; Adams, P., & Novak, M. (2015). *Social justice isn't what you think it is.* Encounter Books; Annan, K. (2016). *Slow kingdom coming: Practices for doing justice, loving mercy and walking humbly in the world.* InterVarsity Press; Barry, B. (2005). *Why social justice matters.* Polity; Bates Clark, J. (2011). *Social justice without socialism.* Createspace Independent Publishing; Bush, G., & and Meyer, R. (2013). *Indivisible: Poems for social justice.* Norwood House Press;

Capeheart, L., & Milovanovic, P. D. (2007). *Social justice: Theories, issues, and movements.* Rutgers University Press; Clayton, M., & Williams, A. (2004). *Social justice.* Wiley-Blackwell; Dewhurst, M. (2014). *Social justice art: A framework for activist art pedagogy.* Harvard Education Press; Eubanks, V. (2011). *Digital dead end: Fighting for social justice in the information age.* MIT Press; Hoefer, R. (2015). *Advocacy practice for social justice.* Lyceum Books; Leacock, S. (2008). *The unsolved riddle of social justice.* Echo Library; Linker, M. (2014). *Intellectual empathy: Critical thinking for social justice.* University of Michigan Press; Miller, D. (2001). *Principles of social justice.* Harvard University Press; Nagara, I. (2013). *A is for Activist.* Triangle Square; Raboteau, A. J. (2016). *American prophets: Seven religious radicals and their struggle for social and political justice.* Princeton University Press; Sensoy, O., & DiAngelo, R. (2011). *Is everyone really equal? An introduction to key concepts in social justice education.* Teachers College Press; Tornielli, A., & and Galeazzi, G. (2015). *This economy kills: Pope Francis on capitalism and social justice.* Liturgical Press; Vogt, B. (2014). *Saints and social justice: A guide to changing the world.* Our Sunday Visitor.

16 Toulmin, S. (1958). *The uses of argument.* Cambridge University Press.

17 The dialogic segment that follows ("Such encounters of possibility always have a beginning…") is the first conceptualization of our collaborative process published as: Alexander, B. K., & Weems, M. E. (2020, November 27). Taking the pulse: Looking for the poetic and performative in terrorism and hate. *International Review of Qualitative Inquiry.* https://doi.org/10.1177/1940844720974109

18 Moraga, C., & Anzaldua, G. (1981). *This bridge called my back: Writings by* radical women of color (pp. 52–53). Aunt Lute Press.

19 Here I am riffing on Madison, D.S.'s (1999) discussion on encountering theory: Performing theory/embodied writing. *Text and Performance Quarterly*, 19(2), 109.

20 Merriam-Webster. (n.d.). *Work.* https://www.merriam-webster.com/dictionary/work; Merriam-Webster. (n.d.). *Enjambment.* https://www.merriam-webster.com/dictionary/enjambment.

21 Winner of the 2018 Best Special Journal Issue Award for (2017). Terrorism and Hate in Orlando, America – Poetic and Performative Responses. *Qualitative Inquiry, 23*(7), 483–571. (Coedited with Mary E. Weems and published by the National Communication Association, Ethnography Division.)

22 See Goltz, D. (2017). The nonsense. *Qualitative Inquiry, 23*(7), 483–571.

23 Hamera, J. (2007). *Dancing communities: Performance, difference and connection in the global city.* Plagrave MacMillan.

24 See Alexander and Weems (2017), pp. 493–494.

25 Also see Prendergast, M. (2015). Poetic inquiry, 2007–2012: A surrender and catch found power. *Qualitative Inquiry, 21*, 678–685.

26 In asking this question, we draw from Hamera, J., & Conquergood, D. (2006). Performance and politics: Themes and arguments. In D. S. Madison & J. Hamera (Eds.). *The SAGE handbook of performance studies* (pp. 421–422). SAGE.

27 See Pollock, D. (1998). Performative writing. In P. Phelan & J. Lane (Eds.). *The ends of performance* (pp. 90–95). New York University Press.

28 Madison, D. S. (2005). *Critical ethnography: Method, ethics, and performance* (pp. 191–198). SAGE.

29 Here I am drawing from resent interest in the relationship between the yin and the yang, and the interpenetration of stillness and activity. Adler, J.A. (1999, March 15). The interpretation of stillness and activity in Chu Hsi's Appropriation of Chou Tun-i. *Kenyon College.* https://www2.kenyon.edu/Depts/Religion/Fac/Adler/Writings/ChouChu2.htm.

30 "Merriam-Webster. (n.d.). *Poetic.* https://www.merriam-webster.com/dictionary/poetic. Merriam-Webster dictionary defines "poetic" as "of, relating to, or characteristic of poets or poetry.

31 I am using this evocative phrase from Kate Chopin's short story, "The Story of an Hour." Chopin, K. (1984, April 19). The story of an hour. *The Kate Chopin International Society*. https://www.katechopin.org/story-hour/.
32 These were the key questions that appeared in the Call for Papers, and included as the framing device of the Alexander and Weems (2017) Special Issue, p. 483.
33 Pollock (1998), p. 96.
34 The italicized constructions in this second section reference themes and constructions that appear in the Special Issue (2017).
35 Hamera, J. (2017). Dancing, Reaching. *Qualitative Inquiry, 23*(7), 545.
36 Here, I am making a reference to the preface of Silverstein, S. (1979). *Different Dances*. HarperCollins.
37 Goltz, D. (2017). Non-Sense. *Qualitative Inquiry, 23* (7), 489.
38 Merriam-Webster. (n.d.). *Spirit*. https://www.merriam-webster.com/dictionary/spirit.
39 Merriam-Webster. (n.d.). *Writing*. https://www.merriam-webster.com/dictionary/writing.
40 Between this essay's writing and publication, we have completed a book-length project. Alexander, K. A., & Weems, M.E. (2021). *Still hanging: Using performance texts to deconstruct racism*. Brill | Sense Publishing.
41 See Diversi, M., Gale, K., Moreira, C., & Wyatt, J. (2020). Writing with: Collaborative writing as hope and resistance. *International Review of Qualitative Research*. https://doi.org/10.1177/1940844720978761. The abstract for this essay begins with a similar take on collaboration in academia, but I believe that I am taking this in a different direction that is linked with administrative collaboration.
42 See Myers-Briggs Type Indicator. In *Wikipedia*.https://en.wikipedia.org/wiki/Myers–Briggs_Type_Indicator.
43 Wright Mills, C. (1959). *The sociological imagination*. Oxford University Press.
44 I use the construction of "information, formation, and transformation" as affirmation of the "education of the whole person" component of the Loyola Marymount University mission, which is grounded in the social justice. See Loyola Marymount University. *Education of the whole person*. The Mission Statement. https://mission.lmu.edu/mission/missionstatement/educationofthewholeperson/.
45 King Jr., M.L. (1963, April 16). *Letter from a Birmingham Jail*. (2018 Penguin Classics Edition). Penguin; Popova, M. Martin Luther King. Jr. on justice and the four steps to successful nonviolent resistance. *Brain Pickings*.https://www.brainpickings.org/2015/03/18/martin-luther-king-letter-from-birmingham-city-jail/.
46 Chang, H., Ngunjiri, F.W., & Hernandez, K.C. (2013). *Collaborative autoethnogrpahy* (p. 17). Left Coast Press.
47 Alexander, B.K., Stephenson-Celadilla, A. E., Alhayek, K., Twishime, P.I., Sutton, T., Hernandez Ojeda, C., & Moreira, C. (2019). 'I'm sorry my hair is blocking your smile': A performative assemblage and intercultural dialogue on the politics of hair and place. *International Review of Qualitative Research, 12*(4), 339–362; Alexander, B. K., Moreira, C., & Kumar, H. S. (2015). Memory, mourning and miracles: A performance script on triple-autoethnography. *International Review of Qualitative Inquiry, 8* (2), 229–255; Kumar, H.S., Alexander, B. K. & Moreira, C. (2013). Legacies of functional (Il)literacy: Triple autoethnographic reflections on finding voice(s) in academic and everyday life. *Liminalities: A Journal of Performance Studies,* 9(3); Alexander, B. K., Moreira, C. & Kumar, H. S. (2012). Resisting (resistance) stories: A tri-autoethnographic exploration of father narratives across shades of difference. *Qualitative Inquiry*, 18(2), 121–133. Doi:10.1177/1077800411429087; Wyatt, J., Ken Gale, K., Gannon. S., & Davies, B. (2011). *Deleuze & collaborative writing: An immanent place of composition*. Peter Lang; Gale, K., Pelias, R.J., Russell, L., Spry, T., & Wyatt, J. (2012). *How writing touches: An intimate scholarly collaboration*. Cambridge Scholars Publishing; Chang, H., Ngunjiri, F.W., & Hernandez, K.C. (2013). *Collaborative*

autoethnography. Left Coast Press; Gale, K., & Wyatt, J. (2009). *Between the two: A nomadic inquiry into collaborative writing and subjectivity* . Cambridge Scholars Publishing; Diversi, M., & Moreira, C. (2018). *Betweener autoethnographies: A path towards social justice*. Routledge; Diversi, M. & Moreira, C. (2009). *Betweener talk: Decolonizing knowledge production, pedagogy, and praxis*. Left Coast Press; Diversi, M., Gale, K., Moreira, C., & Wyatt, J. (2020). Writing with: Collaborative writing as hope and resistance. *International Review of Qualitative*. https://doi.org/10.1177/1940844720978761.

48 Foss, K. A. (1989). Feminist scholarship in speech communication: Contributions and obstacles. *Women's Studies in Communication, 12*, 1–2.

49 See a range of sources, including: Bowles, G., & Klein, R. D. (1983). *Theories of women's studies*. Routledge & Kegan Paul; Bowles, G. (1984). *Strategies for women's studies in the 80s*. Pergamon Press; Aaron, J., & Walby, S. (1991). *Out of the margins: Women's studies in the nineties*. Falmer Press; Hinds, H., Phoenix, A., & Stacey, J. (1992). *Working out: New directions for women's studies*. Falmer; Rao, A. (1991). *Women's studies international: Nairobi and beyond*. Feminist Press; Macdonald, A. A., & Sánchez-Casal, S. (2002). *Twenty-first-century feminist classrooms: Pedagogies of identity and difference*. Palgrave Macmillan; Montgomery, F., & Collette, C. (1997). *Into the melting pot: Teaching women's studies in the new millennium*. Aldershot; Crabtree, R., Sapp, D. A., & Licona. A. D. (2009). (Eds.). *Feminist pedagogy: Looking back to move forward*. Johns Hopkins University Press.

50 See Foss, S., & Griffin, C. (Eds). *Inviting understanding: A portrait of invitational rhetoric*. Rowman & Littlefield. This is 25-year retrospective on "invitational rhetoric" includes: Alexander, B. K. & Hammers, M. (2020). An invitation to rhetoric: A generative dialogue on performance, possibility, and feminist potentialities in invitational rhetoric (pp. 231–246). Republished from (2019) *Cultural Studies ⟷ Critical Methodologies, 19*(1), 5–14.

51 Rosenberg, M.B. (2015). *Nonviolent communication (A language of life)*. PuddleDancer Press. See also Nonviolent communication. In *Wikipedia*.https://en.wikipedia.org/wiki/Nonviolent_Communication. Nonviolent communication is also referred to as "compassionate collaboration" and "collaborative communication."

52 Wilkerson, I. (2020). *Caste: The origins of our discontents*. Random House.

2

EXPLORING SELF WITH/FOR OTHERS

Bryant Keith Alexander

An Ideological Foray on the Politics of the Possible Through Autoethnographic Performance and Spirit-Writing

Prologue[1]

I have been thinking about spirit-writing as a means of drawing upon that which sustains our soul, or that which motivates our momentum to change, or that which defines our commitments in relation to others – through writing, with spirit.

And I have been thinking about the ways in which we evidence the labor of spirit-writing, and why I continue to do the work.[2] In addition to the scripting of a performance, what appears as stage directions provides an interanimating argument of the performance in writing to/with the reader. This represents a further effort to document *spirit-writing as an ideological performance.* Such performance seeks to foreground not merely its substantive content, but also the social, cultural, and political context in which that content is expressed. It consists of writing that shows rather than just telling. The ideological performance "is the way one 'codes' one's ideology into behavior and aesthetics in a way that can then be read and interpreted by others based on knowledge of the referenced meaning systems."[3] Spirit-writing emanates from places of the soul, not just as academic endeavor, but as a survival technique that sustains the spirit of living and the cultural work of scholarship. Spirit-writing makes scholarship dance.

In some ways, spirit-writing as ideological performance speaks to the reasoning of performance and performative writing that guides or undergirds the communicative endeavor. In this project, I am also *engaged in citationality as ideological performance*, or referencing a body of published work committed to the

DOI: 10.4324/9781003203520-2

quest of explicating ideology through autoethnographic inquiry: a form of spirit-writing before it was identified as such.

As a professor of Performance Studies, I often have students engaged in a reflective assignment. I ask them to articulate why they made certain choices in their performance, and what motivated their actions – not just what the body did, or what was the interpretative turn of a phrase. I am asking them: What moved you in the moment? What moved you to action? What turned in you to address this text to project this message? How does this piece, whether found or created, speak to your spirit?

This essay further exemplifies my own choices in using performance as argument, offering an example of the construction of an argument in performance. It integrates those logics within a performance script for the reader as a textual simulation that is not equal to – but instead, referential towards – the live performance. It also furthers what Della Pollock describes when she writes, "performative writing answers discourses of textuality not by recovering reference to a given or 'old' world but by writing into a new one."[4] Her construction furthers my own orientation toward situating myself in the historical present and performing toward future possibilities "centered on the principles of transformation and transgression, dialogue and interrogation, as well as acceptance and imagination."[5] For me, these are terms of the spirit seeking an outlet of possibility. The performer speaks to answer the question about his own continued engagement with performance and performative spirit-writing through autoethnography. He seeks to embody the spirit of being and doing in his response – and of engaging his work as a collaborative partner and exemplar of a thing done.

***

A Performative Response

[The performer speaks.]

Performance and the work of autoethnography have always been, for me, an opportunity: an observation, an outlet, an outreach. Maybe they are a set of tactics and techniques that move me toward the possibility to open up spaces of seeing, knowing, and showing through the articulate and articulating body: a way of exploring *self with and for others*.[6] My logics have been informed in part by what Judith Hamera describes as building *templates of sociality* that help me to render both extraordinary and everyday aspects of living as "readable," as well as "re-organizing the relationships in which these readings can occupy" to make the knowing and politics of being accessible to self and others.[7]

Performance affords me one approach to a *criticality of the self in culture*, which is my operational orientation to doing autoethnography. Aided by D. Soyini Madison's articulation of "critical" in critical ethnography, for me, performance – and performance autoethnography specifically – becomes an act of critical discernment. It forms a conscious process of examining experience and action, a volleying between several positions and possibilities of knowing – each with potentially good outcomes for self and others – followed by a plan of productive action.[8]

> Helping me "to articulate and identify hidden forces and ambiguities that operate beneath appearances;"
>
> Helping me "to guide judgments and evaluations emanating from our discontent;"
>
> Helping me "to direct our attention to the critical expressions within different interpretive communities relative to their unique symbol systems, customs, and codes;"
>
> Helping me "to demystify the ubiquity and magnitude of power;"
>
> Helping me "to provide insight and inspire acts of justice;" and
>
> Helping me "to name and analyze what is intuitively felt."[9]

By analyzing and articulating the available data, I achieve a desired feltness of being whole in the complex intersectional aspects of my identity. I use auto-ethnography as an autobiographical form in which "the self is the source of the system of which it is a part, creat[ing] what it discovers, and although it is nothing unto itself, it is the possibility of everything for itself" in a cultural context.[10]

[*The performer quickly enumerates aspect of his identity, adding the succession of characteristics in a rapid-fire, almost exhausting delivery to further suggest a complexity of self to which all Black people must realize and embody everyday, and to which others must attend beyond the reductivity of race.*]

> For me, as a man
> as a Black/man
> as a Black/gay/man
> as a Black/gay/Catholic/man
> as a Black/gay/Catholic/man/citizen
> as a Black/gay/Catholic/man/citizen/teacher/artist/scholar
> as a Black/gay/Catholic/man/citizen/teacher/artist/scholar/administrator
> as a Black/gay/Catholic/man/citizen/teacher/artist/scholar/administrator/brother-
> Black brother and biological brother, first-generation college student, son of a garbage man; as my mother's son and my father's boy, and always as a child of God.[11]

Each practiced position, portioned and proportionally considered in relation to the whole of my identity, yearns to find and appreciate the tender meeting places – the connections and disconnections in my being. Performance, like *intersectionality*, becomes "a lens through which you can see where power comes and collides, where it interlocks and intersects."[12] I can only maintain a creative life in academia if I recognize that academia can and should be a critical and creative space of possibility in which my intersectional self can be fully alive.

The critical reflexivity of autoethnographic work is not limited to what is assumed to be the private and personal aspects of living, but also extends into the professional and pedagogical spaces of our academic practices. This critical reflexivity is also enlivened by the locational politic of the body engaged in *administrific practices* of higher education – practices that are sometimes both administratively procedural and horrifically challenging to the soul. All of this is held in a tensive relationality of providing faculty, staff, and, most importantly, students with a viable professional, educational, and cultural experience that informs their whole persons in the places of their pedagogical practice.

The practiced place of the Ivory Tower easily becomes an ethnographic site for close study and scrutiny of institutional politics. In these political practices and spaces, my Black male body becomes implicit, explicit, and complicit in all the biases, challenges, opportunities, and possibilities that such spaces present to us all. Hence, I still do the work, even as an academic dean. I do it as an acknowledgement of administration, teaching, and scholarship as informing practices of academic professionalism that hold me in communion with my purpose.

Hence, the performative scholarship that comes from such ethnographic sites is, for me, an embodied praxis with a focus on the tensive relationality of identity markers that are:

> located but not fixed,
>
> listed but not resistant,
>
> comparative but not competing,
>
> with the delimited and exalted aspects of my intersectional self
>
> "as they come together simultaneously to produce social identities and experiences in the social world,
>
> from privilege to oppression" and back again,[13]
>
> in cultural locations as contact zones with differentiated and bifurcated others
>
> compounded in spaces of struggle and danger.

Struggle, as Audre Lorde reminded us: "there is no such thing as a single-struggle issue because we don't live single-struggle lives."[14] *No one does.*

[*The author delivers the phrase, "No one does," both as a statement of fact and as a challenge to the audience (and the reader) to list the elements of their own complex struggled identities and own it, maybe even relative to how Black is often reduced to a singular identity.*]

And danger, because as a Black gay man in America I live in a practiced place, on a continent of danger.

Performance and autoethnographic writing help me through the riots in the streets, and *the riots in my head as* I negotiate the highways and byways of living.

Performance and autoethnographic writing help me to bear the pain and bear witness to the racism in everyday life, even in the Ivory Tower where I seek refuge.

Performance and autoethnography help me to negotiate the disease and dis-ease of these repressive times – the lingering effects of the Donald J. Trump regime, the scourge of COVID-19, and the activism of Black Lives Matter[15] – which are not very different from past times. They're just made more present and potent now, in a different performative confluence of rage, in times of pandemic and the political polarities in which we have to march, again and again, to confirm the complex *matter* of Black Lives.

Performance and autoethnographic writing help me to weave the connective tissue between *protest as performance and performance as protest* in both the public and private domains of my life.[16]

Maybe you have seen that tensiveness in my work over the years

> about race and sexuality in the classroom,
> Or the entanglements of culture in my work on Black hair, barbershops, and salons;[17]
> Or in my work on the sensed isolation in administrative boardrooms; the Black professoriate in the white Ivory Tower, and why I stay to fight and do the work.[18]

Maybe you have seen it in my work on masculinity and being queer – no, that's being racially *quare.*[19]

Or maybe you have seen that investment in my work on class and privilege; the college professor and academic dean who is always

> already the abject body, *the garbage man's kid*[20] – and treated as such sometimes, with my PhD given short shrift in the politics of both elitism and racism in the academy. Though it appears in this current historical moment that the tinted materiality of bodies is now foregrounded to evidence of institutional commitment to diversity, equity, and inclusion. "See, *we have a Black Dean,*" says one of my white colleagues in relation to demands from Black faculty and staff for an increased presence of Blacks in administration.

Or maybe you have seen it in some of my recent work exploring "spiritual strivings" as a

> Black/Gay/Catholic/man in a Catholic Jesuit and Marymount university, and in *the veiled nature of Black life and Black invisibility within society*,[21] and in the work on exploring *queer intersectionalities* and the "impossible purities" of being both particular and plural.[22]

Maybe you've seen it in the current work in which I discuss how Black bodies are "still hanging" on literal and figurative nooses around this country.[23] The work explores the resurgence of the noose in America as an ancient symbol of racism, with strange fruit hanging and Black blood soaking the tree roots. This fruit is not of nature, but of man-made manifestations: a sign, a lesson, and a warning to Black people not to get too uppity (or too safe) in *your/our* freedom in a MAGA climate, which I hope will change soon with our new Pres. Joe Biden. And yet, we bear witness to a range of continued assaults on unarmed Black bodies by police, which has deep historical roots in this country.[24]

#BlackLivesMatters.

#SayHerName.

#KnowTheirNames[25]

Maybe you have seen it in the recent work in which I say, "I need the revolution to be televised now, and you will hear that again and again.

Or in the work that explores *the unbearable lightness of being*[26] and the presumed tensions of

> being a Black gay male, and
>
> being artistic and intellectual,
>
> being an academic and an administrator, or
>
> being Black, gay, and Catholic[27] – these are
>
> old biases of *humans*, not of the universe,
>
> old biases that consistently recur like a straightjacket of expectations relative to the dominant class,
>
> politics of masculinities and performativities mixed with racial privilege and shifting academic expectations of doing more or having to be *twice as good*.
>
> Which, as you should know, has always been a foundational charge to the Black experience in America. It is the lesson that the ancestors taught all those of us who were *young, gifted, and Black*.[28] They said, "You have to be twice as good to be accepted. And then again, know that you will never be accepted as equal."

Yes, our "double binds" are both "ambiguous and paradoxical embodiments" to be recognized and dismissed at the same time.[29] That has always been the Black man's burden – the Black person's burden in America – without choice.

[*Performer presents the following as an aside, maybe as a "stage whisper" as he leans into the audience. The statement serves as historical reminder and a conundrum in the white imagination.*]

For you see, the universe imagined me (us) long before *you/they* were shocked by my (our) arrival on the scene. Though by your (their) own hands you (they) dragged me/us in shackles onto this continent. Only the language of my/our possibility and the closed doors of opportunity lagged behind. Then I (we) was (were) breathed back into being and bequeathed a state of being fully human, again.

[*Performer momentarily pauses, looking at the audience maybe to see their reaction, maybe to allow the statement to sink in. The juxtaposition between "ambiguous and paradoxical embodiments" and "shocked arrival", "dragged in shackles" and "language of possibility."*]

Maybe you have seen that tensive frustration in some of my recent scholarly and creative work where I just let loose my shit, saying overtly what my past work had always said covertly:[30]

> "Fuck you" – I am not what you expected, but I am here.

That work through performance consistently now says,

> I am not what you are most comfortable with at times – but welcome to my world. So, don't apply your self-imposed limitations onto me as critique.

That work through performance and performative writing that used to so *often* be expressed through my signature *eloquent rage*,[31] only now to say:

> "I am not that sycophantic Black boy of your historical reimagination, or the ineffectual faggot that you secretly desire. James Baldwin told me long time ago: *"You have to decide who you are and force the world to deal with you, not with its idea of you."* Trust.
>
> I AM the NEO-NEGRO QUARE DUDE – who is living the fucking life anew in *lightness*, not whiteness. So, check yourself.

[*The following line is delivered to the audience as an anticipated response to the previous line, which was not meant to shock, but to illuminate a reality.*]

> "I don't know why ya'll gagging. She brings it to ya' every ball. *By any means necessary*![32]

> Now my brother Charles Nero might say that I'm *signifying*, because that is a Rue Paul quote juxtaposed against a quote from Malcolm X[33]: a co-informing radical queerness and a radical Black activism in a tensive relationality. A Black *quare* representation that my *brister* E. Patrick Johnson might say speaks both across identities and articulates identities as well.[34]

I do the work.

I have done the work through performance for years, knowing that my body is on the line, with different stakes than others experience. I'm subject to a different level of critique about my *critique in performance* and a *performative critique of my person in everyday life*. But I am happy that the most important people – the few who bridge my professional and personal life – recognize, in time, my efforts in the realm of creating and sustaining *generative utopian synergies* through auto-ethnographic performance, for which critique can serve as a space of open possibilities for self and other – for a deep theorizing of self in/as/with/the other.[35] Thus, performance becomes a textual and embodied *tetrad of reconciliation*. The term was coined by John B. Hatch, to define the four cardinal values that must be restored and realigned in the process of reconciliation: *agency, truth, peace, and justice*, with the interior operational necessities of grace, restorative truth, shalom, and restorative justice each serving as vectors of human social engagement. For me, autoethnography is often a process of reconciliation with self and diverse others.[36]

I continue to do the work.

I do the work even outside of invitation, when some people don't always fully recognize the work that I do, but capitalize on it constantly – like all Black labor that goes mostly unrecognized but consumed.

I do the work.

I do the work as a process of *information, formation, and transformation* for self and society.[37]

I do the work for me, knowing that other young Black performance studies artist-scholars will benefit, because suddenly, in Performance Studies it appears that I have become old school.

It appears that I have become one of the Black predecessors and Black ancestors in Performance Studies – along with D. Soyini Madison, E. Patrick Johnson, and *sista docta* Omi Osun Joni L. Jones, as she writes in an "interanimating diaspora of discussing and experiencing black art."[38] And more exactingly from brother Harvey Young, who describes not just Black people in Performance Studies, but Black Performance Studies as, "nuanced critical readings of and savvy theoretical engagements with the enhancement and experiences of race."[39] All, I tell you, leaning into what sista Angela Davis suggested: that "progressive art can assist people to learn not only about the objective forces at work in the society in which they live, but also about the intensely social character of their interior lives. Ultimately, it can propel people toward social emancipation."[40]

Blacks in Performance **Studies.**

Performing Blackness in Performance Studies.

Black **Performance Studies.**[41]

Oh, what great company!

I am honored to join them in their intellectual heft in/as Black academic labor to the discipline (in the discipline, through the discipline, with discipline) as we systematically illuminate and translate Black culture for public recognition, celebration, and sometimes consumption.

We do the work in a voice and style that has necessarily had to be multilingual, multi-citational, multi-referential, and bimodal – through live performance and scholarly publication – with the skill and necessity *to shift* at the drop of a dime to evidence the work. We evidence the meaning and importance of the work to those who presume themselves to be the gatekeepers of performative scholarly excellence. And thus, we show our dexterity and adaptivity at shifting expectations in performance scholarship through social, academic, intellectual, and political realms, which are all sutured together.[42]

But I also turn to listen to the next generation of young Black scholars working through performance and autoethnography. Ones like Jovan Johnson *killing* it through spoken word with themes of masculinity, racism, love, and joy; Amber Johnson *doing the do* in gender futurity, intersectional autoethnography, and African-American communication; and Jade C. Huell embodying Black experience through stillness and critical memory. That is not to forget the important work of Renee Alexander Craft, whose *work examines the relationship among sociohistorical constructions of Blackness, Black cultural performance, and discourses of Black inclusion and exclusion within a hemispheric American framework.*[43] And I recall the work of Aisha Durham, Marquese McFerguson, Sasha Sanders, and Anjuliet Woodruff, who bind the past to an afrofuturism that imagines *autoethnography as Black.* They write:

> To say "Black" is to consider the possibility that blackness can flesh the felt-sense self as a part of the marked cultural body, can story relational experiences that are inventive and transgressive in its work to democratize forms and humanize the other in cocreated encounters, and can serve as an ontology of resistance in which blackness is harnessed to understand the ubiquitous and generative nature of power – the power to shape identity and experience, and the power employed by the autoethnographer to author or rescript new ones. The ability to conceive creative ways to communicate or convey cultural knowledge across space, body, and time has been a politically imaginative, life-sustaining technology for the African diaspora.[44]

Ah, yes – they know their history, and they are drawn by a communal spirit of possibility.

The work that they do will change a yet-undetermined but imagined Black futurity.

They force a shift.

Now watch me shift again.

Maybe this time I am making a shift that could be more of a *performative fugitivity*, as brother Bryce Henson writes: a move that "partakes in [an] unpredictable and [seemingly] divergent path to other spaces and possibilities" to present a different form of evidentiary knowledge of being and becoming through performance,[45] showing a reach beyond the possible toward the potential.[46] But now, it is with a conflicted sense of my Black body situated in a cultural narrative to which my own casting will be questioned as either hero or whore. But maybe you will still get my point.

[*Performer embodies a tonal and postural change to signify how Black people shift to adapt to different situations, including shifts in voice and expressive modalities as needed and expected – to pass, accommodate the needs of others, or to get the work done.*]

In my engagement of performance, I still believe in *the impossible dream.*

I still believe in what Dwight Conquergood, a white ancestor in Performance Studies who did work on the streets with the people, illuminated for us, though now it seems so long ago.[47]

[*Performer is asking the following questions in a voice unlike his own: a softer, more urgent voice, anticipating his introduction of Aldonza*].

> Do you remember?
>
> Please try to remember.
>
> You have to remember.

Oh, wait! Wait! [*The performer acknowledges this with a playful realization.*]

I believe that I have now slipped into *Man of La Mancha* and the character of Aldonza telling Don Quixote that he has to remember. Not just the quest, or the lyrics to "The Impossible Dream," but to engage the *power of performance* to RE-MEMBER himself to wholeness, and to make possible the dream of living and being fully alive – even when her Lord is not well.[48]

For me, it is SHE, Aldonza, who is also telling HIM, Don Quixote del la Mancha, to continue believing in the power of performance, maybe in the processes of *making belief* and *making believe* in a quest to heal himself and the world[49] – even when he is thought to be mad. In the process, others come to understand the possibilities of living through performance.

And for her own investment, as I believe audiences of performance often beckon, ALDONZA sings, [*as does the performer in performance*]:

> Dulcinea... Dulcinea...
> Won't you please bring back
> The dream of Dulcinea...
> Won't you bring me back
> The bright and shining glory
> Of Dulcinea... Dulcinea...

[*Performer shifts into a didactic, teacherly tone to inform those who may not recognize the literary and performative script that he is referencing to make his point.*]

You do know what I am talking about – right?

See, in the musical play, *Man of La Mancha*, Aldonza is a character: a serving woman and part-time prostitute. But she is also the audience for spectacular performances by Don Quixote in the world of the musical play. In the song she sings, she is yearning for the refined and imagined image of herself as a lady named Dulcinea that Don Quixote illuminates in performance. Like most of us, she yearns for renditions of herself made possible by others, as these selves are activated in others' mad striving and search for sense-making, especially in the performance of auto/ethnography.

And we, like Aldonza, witness and revel not just in their artistry, but at our own invoked possibilities to see and be seen by the world anew in the sometimes divine and idealized essence of ourselves that is made manifest in their performance.[50]

So, as a benefactor of that imaged possibility of herself, Aldonza-as-Dulcinea is really reminding him of the power of performance that has held his mind steadfast and presented her as an elevated being. And DON QUIXOTE de la Mancha, the performer, the dreamer, the mad man, says:

[*The performer assumes the character of* DON QUIXOTE *de la Mancha.*]

> Then perhaps... it was not a dream...
> ALDONZA
> You spoke of a dream. [*She says,*] And about the Quest!
> DON QUIXOTE
> Quest?
> ALDONZA
> Yes, how you must fight, and it doesn't matter whether
> you win or lose if only you follow the Quest!
> DON QUIXOTE
> The words. Tell me the words! [*He says*]

[*The performer responds to the audience.*]

In the play, Aldonza begins to recite the words to "The Impossible Dream." But here, for my own purposes, I offer you the words of Dwight Conquergood, who was also known for tilting at windmills, describing the critical work of performance. He said that performance exists in the "crisscrossing lines of activity and analysis [...] [performance] as a work of *imagination*, as an *object of study*; [performance] as a *pragmatics of inquiry* (both as a model and method), as an optic and operation of research; [performance] as a *tactics of intervention*, and alternative space of struggle."[51]

And as she, Aldonza, beckons, DON QUIXOTE begins to remember his words to "The Impossible Dream."[52] As he says,

> To [**write**] the unrightable wrong
> To love pure and chaste from afar
> To try when your arms are too weary
> To reach the unreachable star

[*In the following moment, the performer/author breaches the porous boundaries of the performatively embodied (in live performance) and the performatively written (in textual archive) to signal to the live audience (versus the reader) the verisimilitude of the ideologic intentionality between the act and action of performance and performative writing. He says to the audience:*]

And here I must confess *that on paper*, I am intentionally using the word "**write**" in relation to the word "**right**" (to write the unrightable wrong) in relation to the lyrics of the song. I'm making a particular reference to how the lyrics apply for me as the opportunity of performance and performative writing to confront culture, with writing and performance as ways of documenting and rehearsing possibility, promoting protest, and pushing back as a form of resistance. They represent ways of confronting challenges of the seemingly impossible, addressing the dichotomies the song narrates – and which we live in everyday life – including:

> To dream <u>the impossible dream</u>
> To fight <u>the unbeatable foe</u>
> To bear <u>with unbearable sorrow</u> and
> To run <u>where the brave dare not go</u>.[53]

Performance and autoethnography for me, and maybe for Don Quixote – (or the playwright and lyricist) – is a quest. In the song, I believe that DON QUIXOTE states his commitment and his persistence in the madness of performance when he says:

[*The performer narrates the lyrics, but sings the three highlighted lines:*]

> And I know if I'll only be true to this glorious quest
> That my heart will lay peaceful and calm
> When I'm laid to my rest
> *And the world will be better for this.*

That one man scorned and covered with scars.
Still strove with his last ounce of courage.
To fight the unbeatable foe.
To reach the unreachable star.

[*Performer, as himself (or is it Aldonza?) asks to the audience.*]

Do you remember?
Please try to remember.

This, for me, is the radical work – the radical impulse of Performance Studies and my own engagement of performance, particularly through autoethnography as a *performative fugitivity* leading toward a *performative futurity* for self and others. We detour from the present, back to the past, with an eye on the future.

Autoethnography is a kind of reading of the self in the context of culture and the presence of cultural others. I believe myself to be respectful of the relational other in cultural contexts of my own knowledge production, and how others are characterized. Yet, I know that I can be no more true to them (*to this glorious quest*) than I am true to myself in the *telling of the told.*[54] *So that my heart will lay peaceful and calm when I am laid to my rest.* So, in my work, I speak a mindful truth to a pained historical past that is impacting the possibility of our joint current present – and our futures. This is cultural work: work that I believe should be liberating for self and others. It is a performed reflectivity: reflexivity and re-fractivity that pivots on an index point of change, modeled and offered as a generative template for others – both the audience and those implicated in the story – whether they like seeing themselves in that light or not.[55] But I always believe that I am fair in how I remember and experience the realities of a moment. I often perform a grace in rendering a truth that is not about "reading" the other, but a focused, thick description of the context in which things occurred. There is a critical ethic of care, both in process and production, that I hope others would offer me, as I provide opening – nay, an invitation – for others to tell their own stories.

[*Performer then answers his own previous question.*]

I remember.
I also try to **RE**-MEMBER myself through performance,
in everyday life, seeking to resolve the tensiveness between the past and present,
but always holding each in relation to possibility and potentiality.

And that is what performance and performative writing offers me. It is why I continue to publicly unpack my shit in a criticality of the self in culture. working to suture the parts of my intersectional self together through an engagement with performance and performative writing through autoethnography. It is why I offer up writing that is *relational* to an audience that I care about, as well as past–present interlocutors with whom I seek resolution and recuperation; evocative in a sensuous awareness of language and movement, voice and volition, that enacts as it describes; *embodied* as it is performed with an experiencing and felt realism of the known; and *consequential*, embracing an intentional political struggle to change myself and the social environment of my cultural awareness.[56]

I perform always for and toward the possible, and beyond.

[*The performance ends. The Black male performance studies scholar exits the stage.*]

BLACKOUT

Epilogue

I began this performative response by stating: In some ways, ideological performance – or the articulation of the ideology that informs performance – speaks to the reasoning of performance and performative writing that guides or undergirds the communicative endeavor. The same can be said for autoethnography, not only as "an approach to research and writing that seeks to describe and systematically analyze personal experience to understand cultural experience,"[57] but also as a communicative endeavor to share lived experience in a public forum of engagement, whether in print or performance. Autoethnography thus extends beyond a process and product to embody a template of sociality. It is not an occasion for audiences to code on the experiences of others, but a generative device that affords the *reader, listener, viewer, and implicated other* an opportunity to witness how they might begin to delve into their own lived experiences or social conundrums, and thus transform anew their ways of seeing and knowing themselves.

My own integrated approach to performing autoethnography, as both social endeavor and cultural work, goes beyond the sometimes-presumed self-serving naval gazing of autoethnography. It allows me to inhabit a public and political intention of transformation, exploring self with and for others. At the end of each performative engagement, I know that I am a better person – and maybe a better cultural citizen – with something more to offer our collective citizen-making in transforming the self, other, and society.

In my work, my spirit is present in my writing, and my writing is a channel of my spirit. They meet at a convergence: an urgency of survival and renewal on subjects of desperate need, blending and bleeding the borders of academic necessity and the things that most matter to lift my soul and save my spirit. They save my spirit in my academic and personal lives, and in my administrative struggles and my spiritual strivings – all of which are so urgent in my life as a Black/gay/Catholic/man/citizen/teacher/artist/scholar/administrator living in America, now and always.

When urgency meets convergence, purpose can be compounded. Spirit-writing compounds the importance of what matters on a personal level, turning the academic endeavor into a *convergent imagining* in which spirit-writing helps the soul to thrive.[58]

Notes

1 The approach to write this essay is inspired by D. Soyini Madison's (1999) "Performing theory/embodied writing," *Text and Performance Quarterly, 19*(2), 107–124. Because I have such tremendous respect for her, I know that this piece falls short of her brilliance, but the form allows me to get at an embodied response to the call.

2 A short, 8-minute version of this script entitled, "Exploring self, with and for others: a template for continued engagement with performance" was performed on November 20, 2020, at the National Communication Association (Virtual) for a performance panel organized by Tami Spry. The panel, titled "Callings at the Crossroads: Performing Creative Longevity in Academia," had the following Abstract: "The performance scholars assembled on this panel each embody over 30 years of exceedingly influential work in performance studies. Profoundly prolific on the page, stage, and classroom, each will reflect upon the archive, the longevity, and the future of their work in performance studies involving the difficulties, the opportunities, the disappointments, and the promise of living a life in and of performance. How does one maintain a creative life in academia? They will speak from the intersectional crossroads of their careers." The panel included Tami Spry, Craig Gingrich-Philbrook, Lesa Lockford, Bryant Keith Alexander, and Ronald Pelias. In anticipation of NCA, this piece was first rehearsed for a performance at Princeton University in a class taught by Dr. Judith Hamera, but was switched out the day before in favor of a performance of, "The Revolution *Will* Be Televised (With Apologies to Gil Scott-Heron)." The full, 55-minute performance was rehearsed and recorded for a non-public academic collaborative that explored issues of race and representation in scholarly research (October 30, 2020). I thank Judith Hamera for her construction of "citationality as ideological performance" after reviewing the first version of this project.

3 Fuist, T.N. (2014). The dramatization of beliefs, values, and allegiances: Ideological performances among social movement groups and religious organizations. *Social Movement Studies, 13*(4), 430. I begin employing this construction in my work (2020) Still Hanging/On: 'Strange Fruit' and 'Glory' Songs of/as/in Protest (or From Stage to Page: Documenting Ideological Performance). In N. K. Denzin & J. Salvo. (Eds.). *Newdirections in theorizing qualitative research in the arts* (pp. 19–30). Myers Education Press.

4 Pollock, D. (1998). Performative writing. In P. Phelan & J. Lane (Eds.). *The ends of performance* (p. 75). New University Press.

5 See Madison, D.S. (1999). Performance, personal narrative, and the politics of possibilities: Visions and revisions. In S. J. Dailey (Ed.). *The future of performance studies: Visions and Revisions.* National Communication Association. Madison writes: "The *performance of possibilities* centers on the principles of transformation and transgression, dialogue and interrogation, as well as acceptance and imagination to build worlds that are possible" (472). Madison continues: "Dwight Conquergood elaborated on transformation and transgression in his speech at the 1995 Otis J. Aggert Festival, 'Beyond the Text: Toward a Performative Cultural Politics'" (483), which was published in the same volume (25-36). Later in this essay, I make a reference to "information, formation, and transformation," which offers an interpretive framework based on the "education of whole person" in the Loyola Marymount University mission statement.

See Loyola Marymount University. *Our Mission.* https://www.lmu.edu/academics/provost/ourmission/.

6 This sentiment drawn from the LMU mission statement, which references being "men and women, with and for others."

7 Hamera, J. (2007). *Dancing communities: Performance, difference and connection in the global city* (p. 23). Palgrave Macmillan.

8 Because I currently work at a Jesuit university, I am consistently trying to integrate the philosophies of the institution into and through my scholarship as an aspect of performed citizenship. I am using the notion of *discernment* in a sense that is inspired by Jesuit education and Ignatian spirituality. I apply the notion of discernment in performance – and specifically in doing autoethnography – as a conscious process of examining experience and action, volleying between several positions and possibilities of knowing with potentially good outcomes for self and others, followed by a plan of productive action. See Loyola Marymount University. *Ignatian discernment.* https://mission.lmu.edu/cis/ignatianspirituality/ignatiandiscernment.

9 See Madison, D.S. (2005). *Critical ethnography: Methods, ethics, and performance* (p. 13). SAGE.

10 See Nero, C.I. (1991). Toward a black gay aesthetics: Signifying in contemporary black gay literature. In Hemphill, E. (Ed.) *Brother to brother: New writings by black gay men* (p. 236). Alyson Publication. In this essay, Nero cites Cooke, M.G. (1977). *Afro-American literature in the twentieth century: The achievement of intimacy* (p. 21). Yale University Press.

11 A portion of this intersectional wordplay is drawn from my essay Alexander, B.K. (2020). Dense particularities: Race, spirituality, and queer/quare intersectionalities. In Goins, M. N., McAlister, J., & Alexander, B.K. (Eds.). *The Routledge handbook of gender and communication.* Routledge Press.

12 See: Columbia Law School. (2017, June 8). *Kimberlé Crenshaw on intersectionality, more than two decades later.* https://www.law.columbia.edu/pt-br/news/2017/06/kimberle-crenshaw-intersectionality. See also Crenshaw, K. W. (2017). "Mapping the margins: Intersectionality, identity politics, and violence against women of color. In K.W. Crenshaw, N. Gotanda, G. Peller, & K. Thomas (Eds.). *Critical race theory: The key writings that formed the movement* (pp. 357–383). The New Press.

13 As Gust Yep notes, "Intersectionality refers to how race, class, gender, sexuality, the body, and nation, among other vectors of difference, come together simultaneously to produce social identities and experiences in the social world, from privilege to oppression" (86). Yep, G. (2016). Toward thick(er) intersectionalities: Theorizing, researching, and activating the complexities of communication and identities. In K. Sorrells, & S. Sekimoto (Eds.). *Globalizing intercultural communication: A Reader* (pp. 86-94). SAGE.

14 Lorde, A. Learning from the 60's. In (2007). *Sister Outsider: Essays & Speeches by Audre Lorde* (p. 138). Crossing Press.

15 See: Alexander, B.K. (2020, August 21). A welcome, a warning and a wish: On entering a doctoral program in educational leadership for social justice in the year 2020. In *Higher education in the time of Trump: Resistance and critique.* (Special issue). https://doi.org/10.1177/1077800420948086.

16 See Black Lives Matter. https://www.BlackLivesMatter.com; Fuoss, K.W. (1998). *Striking Performances, Performing Strikes.* University Press of Mississippi.

17 Alexander, B.K. (2014). Phantoms, amputations and mournings of Black dreadlocks: (or reentering the barbershop). *Text and Performance Quarterly*, 34(4), 409-415; (2003). Fading, twisting and weaving: An interpretive ethnography of the black barbershop as cultural space. *Qualitative Inquiry*, 9(1) 101–128; (2005). Telling twisted tales: Owning place, owning culture in ethnographic research. In J. Hamera (Ed.). *Opening acts: Performance in/as communication and cultural criticism* (pp. 49–74). SAGE.

18 Alexander, B. K. (1999). Performing culture in the classroom: An instructional (auto) ethnography. *Text and Performance Quarterly, 19*, 271–306; (2011). Bordered and

bleeding Identities: An autocritography of *shifting* academic life. In S. Jackson & R. G. Johnson III (Eds.). *The black professorate: Negotiating a habitable space* (pp. 14–31). Peter Lang Press; (2006). *Performing black masculinity: Race, culture, and queer identity*. Alta Mira Press.

19 See Alexander B. K. (2011). Queer(ying) masculinity(ies). In R. L. Jackson II & M. Balaji. (Eds.). *Global masculinities and manhood* (pp. 52–74). University of Illinois Press. See Johnson, E. P. (2001). Quare studies, or (almost) everything I know about queer studies I learned from my grandmother. *Text and Performance Quarterly*, *21*(1), 1–25; Alexander, B. K. (2017). Queer/Quare theory: Worldmaking and methodologies. In N. Denzin & Y. S. Lincoln (Eds.). *Handbook of qualitative inquiry* (5th Ed.) (pp. 254–307). SAGE.

20 Alexander, B. K. (2000). Skin flint (or the garbage man's kid): A generative autobiographical performance. *Text and Performance Quarterly*, *20*(1), 97–114.

21 See the inspiring text "Of ours spiritual strivings" in DuBois, W.E.B. (1989). *The souls of black folk* (p. 3–12). Penguin Books. See also Dillard, C. B. (2007). *On spiritual strivings: Transforming an African American woman's academic life*. SUNY series in Women in Education.

22 See Alexander, B. K. (2020). Dense particularities: Race, spirituality, and queer/quare intersectionalities. In M. Ni. Goins, J. McAlister, & B. K. Alexander (Eds.) *The Routledge handbook of gender and communication*. Routledge Press. See also Brody, J. D. (1998). *Impossible purities: Blackness, femininity, and Victorian culture*. Duke University Press.

23 See Alexander, B. K. (2020). Still hanging/on: 'Strange Fruit' and 'Glory' songs of/as/in protest (or From stage to page: Documenting ideological performance). In N. K. Denzin & J. Salvo (Eds.) *New directions in theorizing qualitative research in the arts* (pp. 19–30). Myers Education Press.

24 MAGA stands for "Make America Great Again." a clarion call of President Donald J. Trump to a white conservative agenda – as well a white supremacist agenda. See Make America Great Again. In Wikipedia. https://en.wikipedia.org/wiki/Make_America_Great_Again.

25 Chughtai, A. (n.d.). Know their names: Black people killed by police in the U.S. Al Jazeera. https://interactive.aljazeera.com/aje/2020/know-their-names/index.html. See Alexander, B. K. (2020). The revolution will be televised (with apologies to Gil Scott-Heron). *Special Issue of International Review of Qualitative Inquiry: Qualitative Responses/Recovery in Repressive Times*. https://doi.org/10.1177/1940844720974075. (Republished in this volume.) This piece was first performed on October 20, 2020, via ZOOM for Princeton University's Dance 314/American Studies 335/Anthropology 356/Theatre 314 course: *Performance in Extraordinary Times: Documenting and Analyzing the Present*, taught by Dr. Judith Hamera. A special thanks to Dr. Hamera and her brilliant and beautiful BIPOC women students for their warm welcome and critical engagement with the first rendition of this performative scholarship.

26 See The Unbearable lightness of being. In *Wikipedia*. https://en.wikipedia.org/wiki/The_Unbearable_Lightness_of_Being.

27 Along with Dr. Kim Harris, Assistant Professor of Theological Studies; Father Marc Reeves, S.J. Interim Director of Campus Ministry; and John Flaherty, Associate Director of Camus Ministry and Director of Liturgy and Music, I was instrumental in activating the inaugural celebration of Black Catholic History Month at Loyola Marymount University, November 2020.

28 See Hansberry, L. (2011). *To be young, gifted and black*. Signet Classics Reissues. Also see Michelle Obama's 2015 commencement address at Tuskegee University. Danielle, B. (2015, May 12). Michelle Obama's 'twice as good' speech doesn't cut it with most African Americans. *The Guardian*. https://www.theguardian.com/commentisfree/2015/may/12/michelle-obama-twice-as-good-african-americans-black-people.

29 See Peterson, E. E., & Langellier, K. M. (2009). Creative double bind in oral interpretation. *Western Journal of Speech Communication, 46*(3), 242–252.

30 See Alexander, B. K. (2021). *Not a fan letter* (or 'Trigger warning: An autoethnographic rant on Jussie Smollet). In B. K. Alexander & M. E. Weems (Eds.) *Still hanging: Performative texts to deconstruct racism*. Brill | Sense Publishing. A variation of this piece was produced and performed at the May 2019 International Congress of Qualitative Inquiry at the University of Illinois, Urbana-IL on a panel organized by Christopher Poulus entitled, "Autoethnography, Resistance, Engagement, and Hope."

31 See Cooper, B. (2018). *Eloquent rage: A black feminist discovers her superpower*. Picador.

32 The first part of this phrase was popularized by Rue Paul of Rue Paul's Drag Race, but it makes reference to Black, gay drag ball culture and the iconic film "Paris is Burning." See Livingston, J. (Director). (1990). *Paris is burning*. Prestige Films. The second part of the phrase is attributed to Malcolm X, but with a history derived from Frantz Fannon and Jean-Paul Sarte. See By Any Means Necessary. In *Wikipedia*. https://en.wikipedia.org/wiki/By_any_means_necessary.

33 See Nero, C.I. (1991). Toward a black gay aesthetics: Signifying in contemporary Black gay literature. In J. Beam & E. Hemphill (Eds.), *Brother to brother: New writings by black gay men* (pp. 229–252). Alyson Publications.

34 Johnson, E. P. (2001). Quare Studies, or (Almost) everything I know about Queer Studies I learned from my grandmother. *Text and Performance Quarterly*, *21*(1), 1–25. Years and years ago, E. Patrick and I used to playfully use the term *brister*, as in the comingling of "brother and sister." We didn't use it in the reductive sense, which sometimes sees the term used problematically in relation to the notion of "hermaphrodite," but in the most empowering sense of the shared sensibilities of both male and female – along with the liberatory possibilities of being, becoming, and fully presenting oneself.

35 Here I am making a mindful allusion to the deep theorizing that Tami Spry (2016) does in her book *Autoethnography and the other: Unsettling power through Utopian performatives* (pp. 9–19). Routledge.

36 Hatch, J. B. (2020). *Speaking to reconciliation: Voices of faith addressing racial and cultural divides* (pp. 9–19). Peter Lang.

37 See Loyola Marymount University. *Our mission*. https://www.lmu.edu/academics/provost/ourmission/.

38 Jones, O. O. J. L. (2020). The brother/sister plays and the Black real. In S. Luckett, D. Roman, & I. Wooden (Eds.). *Tarell Alvin McCraney: Theater, performance, and collaboration* (p. 167). Northwestern University Press. Here I am also making a reference to Jones' (1997) Sista docta': Performance as critique of the academy. *TDR*, *41*(2), 51–67.

39 Young, H. (2013). Black performance studies in the new millennium. *Theatre Journal*, 65(2), 289.

40 Davis, A. Y. (1990). *Women, culture, and politics*. Vintage Books. I have also seen this quote attributed to Salvador Dali.

41 Johnson, E. P. (2005). Black performance studies: Genealogies, politics, futures. In D. S. Madison & J. Hamera. (Eds.). *The SAGE handbook of performance studies* (pp. 446–463). SAGE.

42 See Jones, C., & Shorter-Gooden. K. (Eds.) (2003). *Shifting: The double lives of black women*. Harper-Collins.

43 See Johnson, J. (2020). *Ain't never not black*. Button Poetry; (2017) *Killing poetry: Blackness and the making of slam and spoken word*. Rutgers University Press; Johnson, J., & Coval, K. (2018). *The end of Chiraq: A literary mixtape*. Northwestern University Press; Johnson, A. L. (2020). *Gender futurity, intersectional autoethnography embodied theorizing from the margins*. Routledge; Jackson II, R. L., Johnson, A. L., & Ribeau, S. A. (2019). *African American communication examining the complexities of lived experiences*. Routledge; Johnson, A. L. (2013). Negotiating more, (mis)labeling the body: A tale of intersectionality. In R. Boylorn & M. Orbe. (Eds.). *Critical autoethnography: Intersecting cultural identities in everyday life*. Left Coast Press; Huell, J. C. (2015). Embodying black

experience: Stillness, critical memory, and the black body. *Text and Performance Quarterly, 32*(4), 380–382; Renée, A. C. (2015). *When the devil knocks: The congo tradition and the politics of blackness in 20th century Panama.* Ohio State University Press; Craft, R. A. (2014). "How does it feel to be a problem?": Edris Cooper-Anifowoshe's adventures of a Black girl in search of academic clarity and inclusion. In E.P. Johnson & R.H. Rivera-Servera (Eds.). *Solo/Black/Woman: Performing global traditions and local interventions* (pp. 167–184). Northwestern University Press.

44 Durham, A., McFerguson, M., Sanders, S., & Woodruffe, A. (2020). The future of autoethnography is Black. *Journal of Autoethnography, 1*(3), 289–296. https://doi.org/10.1525/joae.2020.1.3.289

45 See how my brother Bryce Henson writes about *the critical Black ethnographer and performative fugitivity* in (2019) "Look! A Black ethnographer!": Fanon, performance, and critical ethnography. *Cultural Studies ←→ Critical Methodologies.* https://doi.org/10.1177/1532708619838582.

46 José Esteban Muñoz describes *a utopian performativity* when, writing specifically about performance as constructed in Performance Studies, he explains: "Performance, seen as utopian performativity is imbued with a sense of potentiality." In building his argument, he outlines how Agamben (1999) notes Aristotle's distinction between potentiality and possibility. He writes: "Possibilities exist, or more nearly, they exist within a logical real, the possible, which is within the present and is linked to presence. Potentialities are different insofar as while they are present, they do not exist in present things. Thus, potentialities have a temporality that is not in the present but, more nearly, in the horizon, which we can understand as futurity. Potentiality is and is not presence and its ontology cannot be reduced to presentness" (10–11). Muñoz's construction is a stage for building an argument about the residual traces and potency of performance and performative effect, after the fact of audience engagement. See Muñoz, J. E. (2006). Stages: Queers, punks and the utopian performative. In D. S. Madison & J. Hamera. (Eds.). *Handbook of performance studies* (pp. 9–20). SAGE.

47 Conquergood, D. (2013). *Cultural struggles: Performance, ethnography, praxis.* University of Michigan Press.

48 See Martin, A. (1993). The power of performance. In F. C. Corey. (Ed.). *HIV education: Performing personal narratives.* Proceedings of a Conference Funded by the U.S. Centers for Disease Control and Prevention and Arizona State University (pp. xii–xviii).

49 See Schechner, R. (2013). *Performance studies: An introduction* (p. 43) (3rd ed.). Routledge.

50 See Bausch, W. J. (1999). *The yellow brick road: A storyteller's approach to the spiritual journey* (p. 20). Twenty-Third Publication.

51 Conquergood, D. (2002). Performance studies: Interventions and radical research. *TDR, 46*(2), 152.

52 Wasserman, D. (1966). *Man of La Mancha: A musical play.* Random House, Clean & Tight Contents Edition.

53 See ST Lyrics. *The impossible dream lyrics – man of La Mancha.* https://www.stlyrics.com/lyrics/bestofbroadway-americanmusical/theimpossibledream.htm.

54 Pollock, D. (1990). Telling the told: Performing 'like a family.' *The Oral History Review, 18*(2), 1–36.

55 See how I define the purpose and function of "generative autobiography" in Alexander, B. K. (2000). Skin flint (or the garbage man's kid): A generative autobiographical performance. *Text and Performance Quarterly, 20*(1), 97–114.

56 Here I am referencing D. Soyini Madison's (2019) *Critical ethnography: Mode, ethics, and performance.* (pp. 191–199). SAGE. In writing on the evocative nature of performative writing "that enacts as it describes," Madison references Denzin, N. K. (1997). *Interpretive Interactionism* (second ed.). SAGE; and Denzin, K.N. (2003). *Performance ethnography: Critical pedagogy and the politics of culture.* SAGE. The bulk of Madison's

theorizing on performative writing is based in the work of Pollock, D. (1998). Performing writing. In P. Phelan & J. Lane (Eds.). *The ends of performance* (pp. 73–103). Pollock outlines the key features of performative writing, which is: evocative, metonymic, subjective, nervous, citational, and consequential.

57 Ellis, C., Adams, T. E., & Bochner, A. P. (2011). "Autoethnography: An overview" [40 paragraphs]. *Forum Qualitative Sozialforschung / Forum: Qualitative Social Research, 12*(1). http://nbn-resolving.de/urn:nbn:de:0114 fqs1101108.

58 See the poignant article Lanham, J. D. (2021, February 1). A convergent imagining. *Emergence Magazine*. https://emergencemagazine.org/story/a-convergent-imagining/.

3

SPIRIT-WRITING: CREATING FROM THE COLLECTIVE/ COLLABORATIVE VIBE

Mary E. Weems

I didn't understand this in the beginning, but I've never written anything as an individual. My first poem at the age of 13 was inspired by a fatal accident in front of John Adams, which would become my high school 2 years later. The street in front of the building was divided by two roads going in different directions. The distinction wasn't marked by signs, and apparently a young Black male turned down the wrong side of the street, lost control, and ran into a telephone booth – as I walked past, two white men were putting his body into a body bag. I was saddened by his tragic passing and thought: How could Death be so mean?

When I got home, I got a piece of paper and wrote a poem about Death as a scary person who creeps up on your life and snatches you away, and also expressed its inevitability. The poem, which I still remember, ends, "No matter what we grow to be, no matter young or old, we all become part of eternity, for Death never grows old."

Beginning with "Death," writing has always been an organic, spiritual process for me, and once something sparks my imagination-intellect, I'm always trying to write what comes in that moment on the creative vibe, rather than consciously focusing on what I want to say. Once I'd written my first poem, I was writing poetry on a regular basis, keeping my drafts in black and white composition notebooks, stacked in an Amazon puzzle box that granny once gave me as a gift, and only sharing them with either my granny or my sisters and brother. I did this for 20 years. Back then my writing was prompted in two areas: to learn to like/ love myself, and to honor what was happening to Black folks I knew and had never met in the late 1960s. I am blessed to have learned to love myself a long time ago, but honoring the dead Black people, confronting racism, class, and social injustice, remain lifelong themes in my work – and, once I became aware, sexism and LGBTQ issues as well.

DOI: 10.4324/9781003203520-3

When I was 33, I registered for what I thought was going to be a Creative Writing class at Cleveland State University, where I subsequently earned my undergraduate and Masters' degrees. At the time, my plan was to finish my undergraduate degree and apply to law school. The professor teaching the class was Nuala Archer. It turns out the class was about literary analysis, but something in the vibe between us made me go home and type up ten pages of my work which I shared with her next class. At the end of the following session, she asked me to come to her office and told me something that changed the course of my life. She said I had my own voice, that I had talent. She asked: "Now what are you going to do with it?"

All these years later, I can still remember the joy I felt when a professor and professional poet acknowledged my talent and suggested I might be able to find a way to make creative writing a career.

From that day forward, I began sharing my work loudly at poetry readings, sending it out for publication. I joined a writers group, and any time I could take a creative writing course and/or workshop, I was there as part of my commitment to developing my craft.

The second most important course I took as a creative writer was during my senior year. Sandra Halem, a professional playwright who later became my mentor and friend, taught a course titled, "An Introduction to Playwriting." She introduced us to her "free writing" process in the first class. Free-writing means to write as quickly as possible without thinking, to let what comes, come, without going back to re-read, add punctuation, or change anything. She would time us and walk quietly around the room as we wrote, encouraging us to stay in the moment and immerse ourselves in the process. The first time I tried it, it worked. I couldn't articulate it at the time, but I moved into a space between the conscious and unconscious, allowing my pen to write and write and write, staying open to "who" had something to say. When she gave us the prompt, she said we might be surprised by what we wrote – she was correct, I was. It read as if someone else had written it, just like each time I've written creatively. I think this is because thanks to my maternal grandparents, I was raised to have a Black collective rather than individual mindset; to see myself as part of every Black person who's ever lived; to understand that we're stronger together, and that working as a collective gives us a better chance of overcoming racial adversity, and better connects us to our African ancestors.

Like my coauthor, I believe, whether acknowledged or not, all Black people who use written language as their mode of expression use the spirit-writing method. Four hundred and one years of race hatred, blatant violence, and systemic oppression have resulted in our holding on to a strong connection to God and expressing our experiences in ways that allow us to document, inform, rant, vent, protest, demand, and express empathy and, simultaneously, a desire to heal.

Each time something major happens in my life or society at large, my first impulse is to write about it. Occasionally, my subject is violence against each other. For example, when serial killer Anthony Sowell, a Black man, murdered 11 Black women on Imperial Avenue in my old neighborhood, I wrote a play titled "MEAT," all caps, representing my shouting about the way this Black man treated these women like meat; the fact that there was/is a Black-owned sausage making business close by; and how each time the police were called, they claimed to smell rotting meat, even though all of the women – with the exception of one whose "head" alone was found in a bucket in the basement – were buried on his property. "MEAT" because Sowell actually used to have barbecues on his tree lawn for his neighbors. While I was spirit-writing, I stayed in the in-between place that allowed everyone, including the killer, to have their say, and when I went back and read what I wrote, with each of them sharing, it read like someone else had written it.

After the foreclosure crisis hit and Black people were targeted for sub-prime loans, I wrote a body of work on the subject that included a play written in the voices of the objects left behind in the house, a chapbook-length collection of poems titled "Closure," and a full-length collection of poems titled "For(e)closure." In all cases, I practiced spirt-writing, collaborating with the "people" who'd left behind the objects so I could tell their stories. I imagined what it would be like to lose your home as I wrote poetic monologues that were either inspired by stories I was told by friends and family, stories I read, or the stories that came through me in the moment.

During the Trump era (4 years which felt like 100) I regularly wrote when I was so upset, I felt something I rarely feel for longer than a short period of time – hopelessness. I used spirit-writing to express my outrage, shock, and dismay that a country I thought was doing at least a little better as a whole around issues of race, was not. Some of those poems were actually about trying to empathize with someone I refused to let myself hate, as a way of better understanding how a white man who displays the degree of ignorance and inhumanity I witnessed could be elected president of the United States. Some of the poems were about documenting incidents like the time he pointed to one of the few Black men in the audience and said, "Look at my African-American over there," as if he was his Massa. Some of the poems were about protesting an endless series of actions against Black people, women, LGBTQ folks, and members of any other group who didn't kiss the ring and/or ass of the man behind the curtain.

Being able to practice collective spirit-writing, and now collaborative spirit-writing on the vibe, has helped me live fully in the world, including being as happy and optimistic as possible, because instead of holding in my emotions around injustice, I let them out on the page. I clear a space inside me to heal, and hopefully share something that will assist other Black folks in either feeling my connection to them as a Black woman or, if the reader is part of another race/ethnicity/culture, better understanding what I'm writing about so they can learn to empathize and hopefully think more critically about the Black experience.

Working with my brotha-colleague-friend Bryant on this project has added another welcome, exciting dimension to what it means to spirit-write. Instead of channeling spiritual ancestors, people I've never met, I have a partner in the process who brings his spirit, creative vibe, writing ability, ideas, experiences, and ancestors into a collaboration that's allowed us to inspire each other, write pieces together, and respond to each other's work adding, interesting and important layers to this book. It has also been productive to divide the labor with someone I trust completely, a kindred spirit committed to a shared goal.

4

SUGGESTIONS TO FURTHER ENGAGE WITH THIS BOOK

Mary E. Weems

In the preceding entries, we have introduced varying constructions and definitional frames that inform the notion of *collaborative spirit-writing*, along with a series of commitments and basic keywords that undergird this emerging methodology. The following sections of the book are organized around five major themes: revolution, resistance, reimagining, reparations, and redemption. The alliterative play of the section headers is both an extension of the sometimes poetic writing in this project, while also speaking to divisions of labor, as well as what the coauthors see as key performative practices in the struggle of everyday Black lives.

Each section header splays open the theme through the collaborative voice of the coauthors. The languaging of these sections was designed to stimulate thoughts and to ask questions, but not offer answers. We strongly believe that artistic creations are open to the interpretation of each reader who engages with the work, based on what each reader brings to the piece and grounded in their own lived experiences and cultural lenses. We don't want to provide a definitive interpretation that restricts the meaning to what we think each audience member should take from (or bring to) each section. We provide guides, but we invite each reader to engage with the work:

- With an eye to the constructions of each piece: the themes, characters, situations, subjects, voices, historical timelines, and forms.
- With a recognition that each piece is written in ways that are both particular and plural: particular to the experiences of the coauthors in dialogical play with each other, and plural relative to the experiences with which diverse readers might enter or recognize themselves or others.

DOI: 10.4324/9781003203520-4

- With an understanding that while experiences might differ for each reader, the texts also serve as a template on which each reader might begin to write through their own spirit.

The pieces that we offer in each section then serve multiples purposes. We invite the reader to spend some time with each as exemplars of collaborative spirit-writing, while recognizing that:

- Each piece is drawn from the authors' actual lived experiences and perceptions.
- Each piece is written from the particular standpoint of the author while also inviting the reader to locate themselves in the story.
- Each piece leaves a place for contradiction and argument, inviting readers to agree, disagree, or build their own argument of/through experience.
- Each piece stands alone but in a collaborative dialogue between the co-authors. At times the collaboration is integrative to an individual piece. At times the pieces speak to/at/against each other in an order of sequence within the sections. But also, look between the lines and see how the co-authors offer multiple templates of collaborative engagement.
- Each piece stands as evidence in building a broader argument in the book about the struggle of everyday Black lives.
- Each piece speaks to individual experience that always and already implicates others in ways that reinforce that our lives are not experienced in isolation from the factors that shape our experiences: past, present, future.
- Each piece speaks to issues that can be perceived as reductive to **black and white,** but look for the varying shades and particularities of difference to which the pieces allude. The coauthors invite the reader to read, and to definitely write/right themselves into the text.

And if you find yourself negatively implicated in these narratives of experience, how do you respond? Respond in ways that are not just in anger, defense, shame, or guilt. Respond in ways that seek to enact your own revolution, resistance, reimagining, reparations, and redemption. What would that look like and feel like for you – and for others?

And if you find yourself affirmed in these narratives of experience, how do you respond? Well after the sense of personal validation after histories of exclusion and silence of these stories, what's next? We suggest that you roll up your sleeves and begin to be a part of the change that you want to see in the world. How do you begin to right/write as acts of revolution, resistance, reimagination, reparation, and redemption in the struggle to be and become a person with and for others?

- Each piece is grounded in a Black experience from not only two similar but also two very different Black coauthors: straight/gay, married/partnered, parent/nonparent, religious/spiritual, and so on. with all the adjacent and

> extending politics that establish both tensive relations and also evidence the type of collaboration we are committing, toward liberation and social justice. Our collaborative spirit-writing is a template of possibility beyond differences, but grounded in our joint humanity as Black people living in the world.

We suggest that you work your way through this book as you would on a tour through the struggle of everyday Black lives, with the coauthors as guides. Use each section of the book as a series of sites along the way to pause and reflect – to listen to the stories, read the inscriptions of present and past lives, and recognize the historical evolution of each moment and monument to pain and hope. While the sections of this book appear to be separate, as an organizational trope of such projects, the themes (and section headers) of **revolution, resistance, reimagining, reparations, and redemption** bleed through the entire project. None of these are distinctly separate because each is intricately interwoven in a common human struggle. For example, revolution and resistance are tied together, reimagining is a critical component in the impetus and desire of revolution, and reparation is companion to redemption. Move the pieces around, start in any section that moves your spirit, and you will see a point of connection and overlap that creates different configurations in a puzzled picture of possibility. Read yourself into the picture. Write through your spirit and use your spirit to write/right the wrongs and possibilities of our joint futures, anew.

SECTION I

Introduction to Revolution

Bryant Keith Alexander and Mary E. Weems

The original intent in writing this section's introduction was to offer logics outlining what the section seeks to achieve, approach, announce, and engage. But in writing the phrase **"Introduction to Revolution,"** the words took on a broader meaning that extends beyond the pages and constraints of this work, spilling into the historical nature of revolutions.

This project as a whole focuses on aspects of the Black struggle in the United States through the prism of performance, namely performative and collaborative spirit-writing. Yet, the revolution that Black folks seek is not significantly different from that which all oppressed people seek – people who have been denied or denigrated, placed on the lowest rungs of social ladders and held there. Foot to face, chains to arms, and shackles to feet. These are people who have had to revolt and riot as an active performance of outrage, to turn the tides and currents of their social dispositions. They enact revolutionary struggles – including activist marches and mass mobilizations – of like-minded folks who storm seats of government and seats of power. They storm the streets of their discontents, the sources of their pain, in pursuit of the social justice that has been denied to them. They seek to establish a new template of sociality that is not marked in our differences, but in our common commitments to humanity, calling for a new day, new systems of government, and decision-making for a new order.

Revolutions are caused by frustration. They are the people's way of saying, "I am sick and tired of being sick and tired." Of saying, "I am angry as hell and I will not take it anymore." Of saying, "Fuck this shit. Things have to get better." They are a form of asking, "How can I be a part of the change that I want to see!"

Revolutions are the result of an overreached boiling point of economic restraint, alienation, and class striation, overt and unregulated excesses of social injustice, collective resistance, and the confluence of a cultural climate in which

DOI: 10.4324/9781003203520-101

multiple variables collide on a national or international level. Consider, just since the year 2019, the confluence of: the COVID-19 pandemic; the corruption of national and international leaders; the break-up of international unions by political vote, arrogance, and deteriorated relations; the increase of violence against BIPOC (Black, Indigenous, People of Color) and LGBTQ+ (Lesbian Gay Bisexual Transexual Queer populations and our emerging comrades) communities. These are the problematically ideal conditions for revolutions.

Revolutions must be enacted and embodied for spiritual purposes, undertaken on the right side of justice as a response to consistent violence and pernicious indignities. They are not just angry people storming the figurative Bastille to retain their superior positions. There are other names for that shit!

Revolutions must be enacted and embodied for the sake of freedom – for the advancement of human opportunity, possibility, and mobility, and for the release of the mind, body, and spirit before each devolves into acts of self-destruction.

Revolutions must be enacted and embodied as a common cause and caution, with common sense.

Revolutions must be enacted to unleash the global flows of our humanity, activating our abilities to escape our restraints and move closer to our personal dreams and social commitment to democratization.

Revolution is necessary so that the next generation is not socialized into oppression.

5

THE REVOLUTION *WILL* BE TELEVISED (WITH APOLOGIES TO GIL SCOTT-HERON)

Bryant Keith Alexander

When I was a freshman in high school, I went to my first competitive speech event in the category of poetry interpretation. I remember encountering Gil Scott-Heron's now-iconic piece "The Revolution Will Not be Televised."[1] *What did I know, as a 14-year Black boy,* about revolution? Shortly after I began rehearsals, a favorite Black teacher who knew I was using the piece as *the performance of poetry* turned me onto her copy of Scott-Heron's album *Small Talk at 125th and Lenox*. She brought it to school and allowed me to use the album on a record player in the media room of the school library. I was taken by the musical rendition of this already lyrical piece.

I remember that as a 14-year old kid, I struggled with the encoded messages of the text: references like "plug in, turn on, and cop out," and "skag," a slang term for heroin. But I gravitated to the rhythm and cadence of his delivery on the spoken word album. Each expression throughout the song seemed to be delivered on the inhale, on the top of his voice, no bass, as if heightened and excited and exclaiming the words. It was a protest song in which righteous indignation was placed literally against a tribal rhythm that felt like protest – both against Jim Crow laws and the consumerism that blinded the country to the human condition of Black people through media manipulation and promotion of an ideal whiteness. I reveled in the sophistication of his rhetorical moves, in the said and not-said, and the use of the negative (*will not*) as a declarative resistance that became a trope foregrounding the critical necessity of activism.

What did I know at 14 years old when Scott-Heron said:

> *You will not be able to stay home, brother*[2]
> *You will not be able to plug in, turn on and cop out*
> *You will not be able to lose yourself on skag*

DOI: 10.4324/9781003203520-5

And skip out for beer during commercials, because
The revolution will not be televised

It was that the mediatized construction and representation of protests on the nightly news: a rendering of the real, sometimes sanitized, sometimes manipulated, sometimes "the fake news" of the times. Designed to both defend and offend the civil rights cause, the broadcasts reified the social consciousness of Blackness to the established white structural order, offering the choice to view or not to view, to step in and out at will. *Yes – that was then, and maybe now.*

But unlike the negation built into his lyrical phrase, now:

There will be no pictures of pigs shooting down brothers on the instant replay
There will be no pictures of pigs shooting down brothers on the instant replay

His repetition of the phrase almost makes it a double negative, and hence a positive actualization of the real. I see repeated reels of Black people being ritually killed on the nightly news in the year 2020:

> the knee-to-neck technique police officers apply to unarmed Black people.
>
> the chock holds learned at the police academy intended not just to mobilize, but to kill Black bodies.
>
> the billy club beat-downs.
>
> the overt point-blank shootings of unarmed Black male and female bodies being killed by police on the streets and in their (our) own homes.
>
> and the resurgence of Black bodies hanging in town squares and outside Walmart, as monuments to white supremacy integrated with consumerism – all on the nightly news, unadorned and unfiltered.[3]

These killings are juxtaposed by the urgent marching and protests that are mapped and mobilized to protest the loss of particular Black bodies, like, Brianna Taylor, Trayvon Martin, George Floyd, Philando Castile, Alton Sterling, Michael Brown, Tanisha Anderson, Daniel Piude, Atatiana Jefferson, Aura Rosser, Stephon Clark, Botham Jean, Michele Cusseaux, Freddie Gray, Taniesha Fonville, Eric Gardner, Akai Gurley, Gabriella Nevarez, Tamir Rice, Rashard Brooks, and more [*Know Their Names*].[4]

These particular bodies become plural to all Black people, inspiring marches that spread nationwide "from every village and every hamlet, from every state and every city," with the urgent need "to speed up that day when *all* of God's children, Black men and white men, Jews and Gentiles, Protestants and Catholics, will be able to join hands."[5]

It begins to feel that the revolution is being televised. Not as commercial entertainment but as national reckoning.

We know that what is happening on the streets is not exactly transformation, and not equal to actual revolution. The latter is evidenced by changes in systems of government, alterations of the actuality of business as usual, and new ways of talking about the relationship between past, present, and future – a continuum of change and emancipation for oppressed people.

We will not be able to see all of that captured on television and delivered to us in the comforts of our homes, as we're engaged in the domesticities of living, avoiding the social realities of marginalized people and distancing ourselves from the crafted resistance to capitalistic bloat. But in the negative construction of what the revolution will *not* be (televised), the protest song gives fuel to the actual struggle for revolution to which protest marches – bodies on the line – exemplify and advance the struggle to/for revolution.

Protest and activism are the mediums and modalities toward the change that we wish to see. They represent the right-sizing of democracy and the adjudication of crimes of indifference against BIPOC in the United States. Change is made manifest in local impact, and in regional and national elections, with votes turning the tide of leadership in this country as we approach a watershed presidential election – which will be televised.

What I did know as a 14-year Black boy is that the sounds of congas and bongo drums whose rhythms undergirded Scott-Heron's performative spoken word piece were tribal in nature. They signified not only a restlessness, but also a preemptive attack: a striking back and a willingness to fight, with bodies on the line and no holds barred, to reverse the denial of freedoms and end the systematic abuses delivered to Black bodies in the United States. The congas and bongo drums serve as cultural instruments that signify the Blackness of Cuban people of African descent, with origins of the *yuka* and *makut* of Bantu from sub-Saharan Africa, and the *bembé* drums of Yoruba origin from western Africa.[6] Tribal drumming signifies celebration, summons community, alerts others of danger, and activates action. It builds up to the horn that then punctuates the song to trumpet the cadence of the anthem and the march.

What I did know as a 14-year Black boy is that the sound of revolution is tribal.

What I did know as a 14-year Black boy is that if the common people were to rise up in rebellion, outside of the social fear or the social defense of whiteness, there would be no news coverage of the event. My father would say that the white man's position is, "Let the negroes kill each other, then we will just make those who remain clean it up. There is no need to get into their nigga-business until they get into our business." Hence, when I practiced my poetry selection in front of my father, practicing with all the fervor and furry of my 14-year-old self, my father told me, "You got to get mad when you do this piece. You got to get into their business. That is what protest is about. It is not just about our business of getting justice. It is about our getting justice through changing their business as usual – that's when the revolution will be televised and publicized and made known." (And felt in the dailiness of our experiences.) My father was a simple but a complex man, and the piece spoke to him even if I struggled to speak the protest of the piece at the time.

What did I know as a 14-year Black boy? I knew that the reference to "pigs" in the song was a reference to the "police" – the po po – the symbolic, unregulated enemy of protest and Black people – both then and now.

What did I know as a 14-year Black boy? I knew that when the revolution happens, shows like

> "Green Acres," "Beverly Hillbillies," and "Hooterville Junction"

(or whatever their current counterparts portraying nostalgic renditions of white comfort without concern for racial issues, as Scott-Heron writes)

> *Will no longer be so damn relevant*
> *And women will not care if Dick finally got down with Jane*
> *On "Search for Tomorrow"*
> *Because Black people will be in the street looking for a brighter day*

I knew that then, and I know that now, because Black people in the year 2020 are *in the streets [again] looking for a brighter day*. And Black people are challenging the systems on every terrain of their practical and political engagement.

Black people are challenging systems of oppression: challenging systemic oppression in every structure of governmental rule and human social engagement.

Black people are challenging the White Ivory Tower, colleges and universities around the country – those presumed bastions of liberal ideologies that consistently, persistently, and perniciously perpetuate racial bias, even when they celebrate diversity as the hallmark of their character and mission.

Black people are pushing back and questioning the performative realism of commitments to Diversity, Equity, and Inclusion (DEI) initiatives that are neither seen nor palpably felt in their (our) daily lives. We are also dealing with some of the same "well-meaning white folks" who *explicitly* resist DEI initiatives either because they don't want to share the wealth under threat, or because they just don't see the value of DEI relative to their own privileged positionality – failing to comprehend the benefits of equity to our joint humanity and society.

When I reference, "well-meaning white folks," I am invoking the cultural aphorism of those who recognize the viciousness and complicity of their everyday performance of whiteness. These performances of whiteness always seek to maintain social order by placating the other, a sort of "Southern hospitality" for the country. The phrase encapsulates the upholding of an "imperialist nostalgia… governing relations of dominance and subordination" as an idealized relational performative between race and class, regardless of who won the war of aggression.[7]

Hence, I use the phrase explicitly to counter to the apologetics in the rhetorics of "implicit bias," *which refers to the attitudes or stereotypes that affect our understanding, actions, and decisions in an unconscious manner.* It is the "unconscious manner" part of that construction that allows us to avoid accountable for our behavior – providing the excuse, "Oh I didn't realize I was oppressing you." Trust me, I understand the psychological and theoretical logics that undergird this principle. The process and recognition of what informs our unconscious actions is important. Such recognition is a first step in the process of change, and behavioral change is critical. But for me, change must happen without the excuses, because the effects on the ones being oppressed is so overt and palpable in their (our) direct experience. So, let's move the discourse toward active change, recognizing that at times, *explicit bias* is real, and that by any other name it is racism, sexism, homophobia, and more. We must also address that head on.

My father used to tell me, "Just because people are showing their teeth, don't mean they are smiling. Watch out for those well-meaning white folks who invite you in as evidence of their liberalness as they also continue to limit your access, silence your voice, and tie shackles to your mobility." My father taught me that the construction of "well-meaning white folks" is not a reference to just white people. Because there are those (maybe even "those of us") BIPOC folk who are *well-meaning* in our self-identifying as different, and have become comfortable as the systemic evidence of diversity even in our isolation. Such individuals may intentionally (or not) help Prospero rule, serving as gatekeeper and negotiator for racial dissention, while also serving as sacrificial lamb in a broader struggle – or even offering other people of color up for auction.

Sometimes the *well-meaning* place other bodies with other differences on the line, as evidence of their noble worthiness to rule. Or in my own experience as patsy and pawn, they begin *weaponizing their marginality* against other activated racial subjects. This serves to ensure their tensive interests as both privileged and pathologized don't get overshadowed, even when their particularity has often been intentionally deflected in the public domain (e.g., now the emergence of "coming to America stories," or "raised as … stories," or "coming out stories," or "first generation stories").[8] I am all about people speaking their truth, but that truth should be used as illumination for the cause, and not subterfuge in a pale rendition of "me too." Otherwise, it's not about emancipation or reparations – but about diversion from the primary issues of liberation for all.

So, my father was referencing a performance of whiteness – of white politics and white acceptability, both inside and outside of white bodies – that is embedded within institutional practices of being and belonging, in which some BIPOC get trapped as patsy and pawn, creating an internal tension within the blended category of being BIPOC. Many years later, when I became a faculty member and then administrator in predominately white universities, my father warned me of this trap and reminded me that *my presence in those places is not revolutionary; it is what I do in being there that can serve to activate revolution.*

And just as my 14-year-old self struggled with some of Scott-Heron's encoded messages and references – like "plug in, turn on, and cop out," and "skag," the slang term for heroin – I struggle sometimes in decoding the politics of DEI and antiracism rhetoric – though it is not that I don't believe.

BIPOC old and young, faculty, staff, and students at universities across the country, are asking: "What the fuck?!" It is both a question and a performance of outrage. We're saying: Show me the evidence of your commitment.

What does an anti-racist university look like? Does it mean equal pay across racial lines with people of equal qualifications? Does it mean equal representation of BIPOC across all lines of struggle and engagement: students, staff, faculty, and administration? Does it mean equal opportunity for promotion and advancement in the realms that tease at the tensions between equality and equity? Is it compensation for the invisible BIPOC labor in the everyday efforts of DEI Initiatives and the recruitment of other BIPOC folks to the (relative) plantation? What does anti-racism mean as *evidenced action* and *state of being* for the lived experiences of Black, Indigenous, and People of Color?

Maybe it means that "active process of identifying and eliminating racism by changing systems, organizational structures, policies and practices, and attitudes, [will result in the] redistribute[ion of power] and shared equitably."[9]

Such a revolution would supplant systems of power for something that looks and feels more like equity – within a common humanity. Initiatives are good. Evidenced action is better. And to succeed would be a revolutionary act.

Such a revolution needs to be televised, publicized, and promoted as an anthem of freedom and as evidence of a just society. "*Free at last! Free at last! Thank God Almighty, we are free at last!*" is its own anthem – one that is yet to be realized. But I believe that a revolution in action and activism is happening. And it is being televised.

What did I know as a 14-year-old Black boy? When Scott-Heron wrote and spoke:

> *The revolution will not be right back*
> *After a message about a white tornado*
> *White lightning, or white people*

I understood that the revolution would signal a paradigm shift of representation and opportunity.

I understood that the revolution would open spaces of knowing the self as other, and the other as the self. But it is not a declaration of sameness as an amalgam of assumed color-blindness. Rather, it is the true recognition of the power and possibility in diversity – yes, race and difference – and a celebration of the diverse cosmologies of knowing across cultures and gender formations that, when joined in true dialogue, can speak to the world's greatest needs. This is separate from the racial indifference and social injustice that currently exists, where whiteness is foregrounded and repeated as performative preference of the ideal.

Emphatically, Scott-Heron ends his piece by stating:

> *The revolution will not be televised*
> *Will not be televised*
> *Will not be televised*
> *Will not be televised*
> *The revolution will be no re-run, brothers*
> *The revolution will be live*

Scott-Heron suggests that BIPOC folks would not see the revolution on television, because they/we would necessarily be making the revolution, ourselves, in the streets – Live! I believe that for him, "street" was metonymy, and that the liveliness of such revolutionary action must occur in all the practiced places of our labor and anticipated liberation. We can make public the action of revolution by speaking truth to power and broadcasting the needs and actions of change with a voice and volition that fits our manner but makes a difference, both micro and macro, in the places we work, labor, and habitat. *Where you stand is where the line begins.*

***

When I was a freshman in high school practicing Gil Scott-Heron's "The Revolution Will Not be Televised" for a speech tournament, I practiced in front of my father. After his coaching me on voice and tone and passion – and even my use of the little black binder that was *sine qua non* to the performance of literature – my father asked if I would like to perform the piece in front of his friends for an event at the Knights of St. Peter Claver Hall, a Black Catholic men's service group honoring the life of Jesuit Priest St. Peter Claver. They often had events that featured the Black kids in the church performing and speaking liberatory rhetorics. But he wanted me to ditch the physical text and truly embody the performance in word and gesture.

So, I did.

It was a formal occasion, and I wore my new athletic-fit black suit, a white shirt and a thin black tie. My dad picked out the outfit – he thought it made me look both religious and militant, with a formality of appearance that structured my thoughts and made my presence known. It was a mixture between Malcolm X and Martin Luther King. My dad wanted me to live between those two realities.

The performance went well. The audience consisted of Black knights and their wives, and the Lady's Auxiliary (of which my mother was a member) was receptive and responsive. I delivered the piece with passion, and with the right amount of anger that a 14-year-old boy could muster while keeping it believable. At the end of the event, all the students who performed received envelopes with a modest scholarship to support our education.

My father was proud.

My performances during the actual speech competitions went differently. I brought the same fervor and impassioned delivery but was forced to appear before white judges who never quite got it. Or maybe they were resisting the revolution the piece advocated, and which implicated them. After getting lukewarm responses at several tournaments, I changed my program to a collection of poems by Langston Hughes that featured, "The Negro Speaks of Rivers." My rankings went up. Maybe they considered the selections to be more poetic and literary, though the work was no less radical. In particular Hughes alludes to rivers as baptismal, spiritual, and sacred countenance; as sustenance for agriculture, industry, and the fuel for labor; as yearning for adventure and freedom; as sites of struggle for direction, domain, and destiny; and the vehicle for slave trade. Langston was not just a romantic; he was radical. And like him, "My soul has grown deep like the rivers."

I need the revolution to televised, like that night in November 2008 when I watched the televised announcement that Barack Hussein Obama II was elected as the 44th President of the United States, before going on to serve two terms from 2009 to 2017.

I need the revolution to be televised, like the raised fists and one-kneed resistance of national professional athletes who publicly protest and resist against the killing of unarmed Black people in the United States, *home of the free and the brave.*

I need the revolution to be televised, like the efforts and actions of the **BLACK LIVES MATTER** movement on the nightly news. Today, televised activism is penetrating the American sensibility and drawing the most diverse group of people from all races, creeds, and nationalities to the streets in protest, as part of a historic and transformative action rooted in the logic that "WE" cannot say that "ALL" lives matter "Until Black Lives Matter."

And I offer this necessary expansion:

> We cannot say that **"ALL"** lives matter until BIPOC Lives and those who have been historically marginalized and disenfranchised – intersectionally celebrated and yet despised for their lives and identities – also "**MATTER.**" All in God's great design for humanity.

For in the year 2020, the intersectional politics of identities must also be placed on the battlefield for social justice in communion and comradeship.

I need the revolution to be televised for every Black person living, for those still to come, and for the ancestors who are still stirring their support for change through middle passages of pain and promise – and for those who sacrificed their lives in the battle for my civil liberties.

I need the revolution to be televised because right now, "I Can't Breathe." And I cannot hold my breath any longer.

***

Gil Scott-Heron's song lyrics were infused with the social and political themes that advocated, in content and rhythm, the Black militancy of its time. It has become an anthem for generations seeking change, juxtaposing Civil Rights advocacy against American consumerism, which is always a reference to social inequality manifested in buying power, upward mobility, and the sustainability of life – of both living and thriving.

In the title of this piece, "The Revolution *Will* Be Televised (with apologies to Gil Scott-Heron)," the reference to apologies is a stylistic gesture of using his iconic text as a vehicle for my personal protest. I hope that he would say in response, "Cool Brother, no apologies needed. Let's do the work of revolutions."

"Let's make the revolution, LIVE!"

News Release: Joe Biden elected 46th President, United States of America, and calls for "era of demonization in America" to end.

[*Dedicated to the Black Faculty and Staff Association, the #BlackatLMU (Student Alliance), and the BIPOC Alliance at Loyola Marymount University.*]

Notes

1 Scott-Heron, Gil. The revolution will not be televised. https://genius.com/Gil-scott-heron-the-revolution-will-not-be-televised-lyrics.

2 See Woman's body found hanging from tree outside Walmart in Georgia. https://www.cbsnews.com/news/south-fulton-georgia-woman-body-hanging-tree-outside-walmart-police-say/

3 Know their names: Black people killed by police in the us" (a short list). https://interactive.aljazeera.com/aje/2020/know-their-names/index.html.

4 From the Martin Luther King "I have a dream" speech: https://www.americanrhetoric.com/speeches/mlkihaveadream.htm.

5 See Congas, https://en.wikipedia.org/wiki/Conga

6 See Bryant Keith Alexander (2012). Chapter 2: Southern Hospitality Indeed!: A Performative Engagement with Art Depictions of African American Culture in the Rural South. In Bryant Keith Alexander (Ed.), *The performative sustainability of race: Reflections on black culture and the politics of identity* (pp. 53–83). Peter Lang Press. See McPherson, T. (2003). *Reconstructing Dixie: Race, gender, and nostalgia in the imagined south* (p. 9). Durham, NC: Duke University Press). McPherson is referencing: hooks, B. (1992). *Black looks: Race and representation* (p. 173). South End Press. hooks quotes Renato Rosaldo, *Culture and Truth: The Remaking of Social Analysis* (Boston: Beacon Press, 1989.) I re-explore the trope of southern hospitality in the works of Jerry Weems in the forthcoming essay, "Dreamscapes and Escapedreams: An Autoethnography through the Art of Jerry Weems" in an upcoming issue of Departures in Critical Qualitative Research (2021).

7 Thanks to Michele Hammers offering me the construction of "weaponizing marginality" in a ZOOM conversation on October 19, 2020; 9:40 a.m.

8 I am using this definition from the NAC International Perspectives: Women and Global Solidarity). https://web.archive.org/web/20201101022553/http://www.aclrc.com/antiracism-defined.

9 See how I offer an analysis of "The Negro Speaks of Rivers" in Alexander, B. K. (2020). A welcome, a warning and a wish: On entering a doctoral program in educational leadership in the year 2020." Special issue: "Higher education in the time of Trump: Resistance and critique." *Qualitative Inquiry*. First published August 21, 2020 https://doi.org/10.1177/1077800420948086.

6

FREEDOM

Mary E. Weems

When I think about education, I can't write a poem. Somehow metaphor, simile, imagery, all the literary devices used to make something sound better fall away, and I'm left with a lump in my throat, a faster beating heart, tears. Being reminded of the empowering force of a free-thinking and feeling open mind takes me back to all of the conversations I had with Grandpa, who had to drop out of school in the eighth grade because he couldn't see. It was during the depression, so his father was working for food, and Grandpa needed to work too to help the family. Grandpa thought that with enough common sense as a foundation, nothing was more important than a good education: not money, not the things you buy with it, not fame.

I think about all the mornings Mama got up at the crack of dawn to earn sub-pay at the local laundry, burns up both arms like tattoos from the hot dryers, sore feet and sweated out hair from spending her days washing other peoples' clothes.

When I think about education, I think about the two teachers I had who told me I was a poet, that I could do anything I set my mind to, that I could fly if I wanted to. I think about the other teachers who've become one memory I try to forget – the ones who told me I couldn't speak proper English, who ignored my constantly raised and curious hand, and the few who gave me lower grades than what I'd really earned.

When I think about education, I think about ancestors who lost their lives, or were beaten and maimed for learning to read and write. I think of all of the things my ancestors went without in the South after slavery ended to build their own schools, with some promising wages they hadn't earned, all the little money they had, freedom labor.

I think about the Little Rock Nine: nine Black students who faced down government officials, the Klan, violence, and hatred to integrate an Arkansas

DOI: 10.4324/9781003203520-6

school and for a chance at an *un-separate* and equal education. I think about the fact that the majority of urban public schools are re-segregated today. Why?

When I think about education, I think about all of the future educators in this room. Choosing the path of any aspect of education is like becoming part of a huge sacred trust.

Except instead of property, you'll have an opportunity to influence the rich minds and emotions of people. Educators are directly involved in all other disciplines, professions, and trades, because everyone who learns to do anything learns to do it with our help.

This means it's important to give this opportunity your best effort. To learn the value of empathy, compassion, love, and social justice so you can help facilitate this development in the people you will encounter. Too often people focus on economic power; the power of owning and controlling everything. But unlike education, economic power can be lost, usurped, and taken away. Unlike owning *things*, owning your own mind is a forever love affair that doesn't end until your physical self, moves on to what Brother Najee calls "its next transition." A free mind guides a free spirit – a consciousness able to interpret the world from a position of intelligence.

Education is freedom. Educators are like the guides through the Underground Railroad. We help to build communities of learners using mutual respect, reciprocal learning, caring, and sharing as the code words of the song we sing over and over; our mantra; an ongoing, always-learning labor of love that uses everything we know to inspire others to think using their imagination and intellect. To learn all they can, about all they can, whenever they can. To pass it on like my ancestors moved from secret place to secret place, risking everything for one of the most important things worth pursuing.

> "I sit on a Man's Back
> choking him and making
> him carry me, and
> yet assure myself
> and others that
> I am very, very
> sorry for him and
> wish to lighten
> his load by all possible
> means – except by
> getting off his
> back.
>
> *Tolstoi*

I've always strived to represent the future of education. I am blessed to be part of a movement that started centuries ago in the Americas, and around the world: the movement for freedom for *all* people. As educators within the movement, we use our intellectual power to help get those who have colonized the world off of the backs of the oppressed, the have-nots, the folks at the bottom of the bottom. All races, ethnicities, and classes of people deserve a chance at reaching what the singing group the Temptations called "the unreachable stars" of their own life dreams.

Peace.

7

"COMMON SENSE" AND "OH FREEDOM"

Bryant Keith Alexander

Common Sense

> *PERHAPS the sentiments contained in the following pages, are not yet sufficiently fashionable to procure them general favor; a long habit of not thinking a thing wrong, gives it a superficial appearance of being right, and raises at first a formidable outcry in defence of custom. But tumult soon subsides. Time makes more converts than reason.*
>
> *Common Sense by Thomas Paine*[1]

I have a PhD and my father only completed the fourth grade.
My father had common sense.

A garbage man by trade, my father taught me lessons;[2]
lessons for living and navigating the world that both transcended
my fancy education and taught me how to think.
How to think through the sometime morass of higher education
and how to ritually return to the front porch theorizing of my childhood
sitting at his knee. My father taught me how to engage in
deep theorizing from a grassroots perspective as a man, as a Black man.

My father had common sense.

My father had the type of common sense that said,
"Look both ways before you cross the street."

DOI: 10.4324/9781003203520-7

> "Just because someone is showing their teeth, don't mean they are smiling."
>
> "Don't look too long at white women."
>
> "The white man sees you as Black first, and maybe, a man second. And that signals caution."
>
> "I'm sending you to that college, but don't forget where you come from."

My father had common sense.

> When studying at the kitchen table during my undergrad days,
>
> my father would sometime see a puzzled look on my face.
>
> He would ask what was wrong.
>
> He would ask in that way in which parents know how to *read* their child's expression,
>
> even if they could not *read* the textbook in front of them.
>
> I would share with him what I did not understand in my reading of theory.
>
> And he would confidently say, "Oh, I think he is talking about..."
>
> *And he was always right.*

My father had common sense.

> When I had troubles, the kind that little kids have or
>
> the kind that adult Black men encounter in these United States of America.
>
> My father told me stories of growing up as a Black man in the South
>
> through and under Jim Crow.
>
> He told:
>
> *Back door stories.*
>
> *Back of the bus stories.*
>
> *Back to the jungle stories.*
>
> He would tell those stories.
>
> He would *preach* those stories in rapid-fire succession
>
> without pause, as if they were already loaded, and
>
> sitting on the tip of his tongue to shoot (to tell); waiting for an ear to hear.

The stories were about *his pain, scars, and survival.*

The stories were about *how he got over.*

The stories were *about his travels,*

and the lessons always came through.

The lessons always got *me* through those experiences

as a Black boy, and a Black academic man.

Those experiences that were never the same,

and *never not not the same,*

as my father.

My father had common sense.

And in those rare times when I thought about dropping

out of college to work and offset his *Black man's burden,*

my father would say, "You know, you are not too old for me to whip your ass. Let me take care of my own family. Go study."

My father valued education, maybe because he didn't have it,

but more importantly because he wanted me to have it for both of us.

Common sense tempered, but not tampered by academic knowing.

He saw education as an opportunity for *both of us* to get over.

Education as a practice of freedom.[3]

My father used to introduce me to his friends as "Dr. Alexander."

Even before I was a doctor. He willed me into being a professor.

My father had common sense.

And I am still learning.

"*OH* Freedom"[4]

Bryant Keith Alexander and the Ancestors

This is an expression.

This is an exasperation.

This is an aspiration.

This is a Black performance of resistance in the religiosity of faith.

This is an anthem that every Black person knows and sings in the company of *the faithful*;

in church, in the graveyard, in the protest march, and in the dark recesses of everyday living in a still-racist society.

Oh freedom, oh freedom, oh freedom over me
And before I'd be a slave, I'll be buried in my grave
And go home to my Lord and be free

A post-Civil War African-American freedom song often linked with the Civil Rights Movement. But a song that I remember sometimes whispered in my ear as a child at bedtime or wailed into my consciousness as a lesson in both faith and protest. A song sung by the old Black elders at the 6:00 a.m. mid-week mass at Immaculate Heart of Mary Catholic Church, or at Syrie Funeral Home at a Friday night wake, when one of their contemporaries had passed. The song sung as a mournful declaration, prayerful release, and a joyous celebration for those who were *done with the troubles of the world and going home to be with God.*[5]

No more moaning, no more moaning, no more moaning over me
And before I'd be a slave, I'll be buried in my grave
And go home to my Lord and be free

The repetition of the mantra made manifest in a commitment to return and *not to return*, a sacrifice of the body but not the spirit and the soul. A repetition turned reflective and reflexive to the acts and degradations of everyday Slave/Negro/African American/Black living to which positionality led to a performativity of servitude. But not without a resistant soul.

No more tommin'," No more tommin'," No more tommin'," over me
And before I'd be a slave, I'll be buried in my grave
And go home to my Lord and be free

Oh Freedom is a performative, a thing said and done. It narrates salvation, *singing* and *glory, over me* as we continue a performance of resistance to the very end. *And go home to our Lord and be free* as a pathway to freedom; a pathway in resistance to that which has been historically denied us in our living. The song serves as shield, sword, and solace against everyday struggle. These are tools of both faith and war, reaching, as Mary writes and the Temptations sing, for *"the unreachable stars"* of our life dreams. And that is not about *tilting at windmills* in a Don Quixote kind of way; it signals the persistence and resiliency of the Black soul held in a tensive relation to freedom.[6]

Notes

1 Thomas Paine, Common Sense (February 14, 1776), http://pinkmonkey.com/dl/library1/sense.pdf.
2 Alexander, B. K. (2000). Skin flint (or The Garbage Man's Kid): A generative autobiographical performance based on Tami Spry's *Tattoo Stories. Text and Performance Quarterly, 20*(1), 97–114.
3 Hooks, B. (1994). *Education as a practice of freedom*. Routledge.
4 One version of this song appears in *Lead Me, Guide Me: The African American Catholic* Hymnal. GIA Publications.
5 A line from "Song I Will be Done with the Troubles of the World" another African American spiritual made iconic my Mahaila Jackson, https://www.youtube.com/watch?v=gNoxoUX2vqQ.
6 Leigh, Mitch. (1928–2014). *Man of La Mancha: A musical play*. New York: Kapp, 1960–1969.

8

THE DEVOLUTION OF GIL SCOTT-HERON

Mary E. Weems

I was in my mid-20s when I started hearing about crack. Like most bad news, not long after I heard about it, I learned about friends and family who were using it.

A few weeks ago, when I stopped at a red light on my way downtown, I was reminded of what the crack epidemic did to Black communities all over this country. A razor-thin, dark, petite sister – her hair in short, slept-on-hair-knots, her top, bottoms, and shoes forgettable, her eyes the dead of a used crack pipe bowl – almost got close enough to my car to ask for money, but in that moment the light changed. As I drove off, immediately regretting not stopping long enough to give her a few dollars, I started to remember when I used to see cracked-out women (never men) on the streets, smiling wide, switching their behinds like distorted fashion models, trying to attract any man who'd stop long enough to get a blow job in his car in exchange for five to 10 dollars for a rock.

At the time, it was so common that after a while, instead of slowing down, feeling sad and bad for sisters who, there but for the grace of God could have been me, I made myself just glance and keep on with my day as a way of dealing with something I felt helpless to stop and didn't want to witness. Seeing the sister in 2020 also made me think about the fact that crack use has never really left. It is just gone underground, because the stigma behind it makes people as old as me – and older – hide that fact they're still using.

A documentary titled "Crack" explains that in 1980, the drug rushed into our neighborhoods like a killing flood, with the help of the U.S. Government's involvement with Nicaragua and its cocaine trade. The epidemic benefited politicians, corrupt police officers, and Black drug dealers, who learned to cook it down to cheap rocks and sell it to their neighbors as a fast track out of devastating poverty.[1] And until Ronald Reagan started the War on Drugs, they didn't have to worry about the police, who watched the drug deals go down and did

DOI: 10.4324/9781003203520-8

nothing – either because it was Black people and they didn't care, and/or because they were getting paid by the dealers. As the film references, I also remember that young white men from the suburbs would make quick trips to all-Black streets to purchase their crack and leave.

As manifested in our communities, the War on Drugs should have been called the War on Black People, because even though two-thirds of the people using crack were white, the overwhelming majority of people arrested and sent to prison for either possession or selling were Black. And while a small number were women, most were Black men.

Reading the *New Yorker* article that opens this piece, "New York is Killing Me" by Alec Wilkinson, who interviewed Gil Scott-Heron in his apartment several times, I learned that one of my Black Activist heroes – an amazing poet, musician, and self-described "bluesologist," or "a scientist who is concerned with the origin of the blues" – was more devastated by crack addiction than anyone I've ever known. Scott-Heron wrote what I still consider my favorite piece about the grassroots movement for freedom, "This Revolution will not be Televised," in 1968 when he was 19. By age 23, he had written two novels, a volume of poems, and several unforgettable, politically charged songs. These quotes from Wilkinson's article paint a picture, that's hard to see and impossible not to:

> "He lived in Harlem…brown couch covered with burn circles, propane torch on the floor."
>
> **Ironically, I've only written one poem about the crack epidemic, "Fortune 500," which is part of "Closure," my play about the foreclosure crisis told from the perspective of the objects left behind in the houses.[2] The poem is about what happens when a witch casts a spell on an afro and turns it into a brown rug in a crack house, which back then was called "The Enterprise," because when you smoked rock you were beamed up.**
>
> "He was thin then, but now seems strung together from wires and sinews…he looks like bones wearing clothes."
>
> "He doesn't like to look in mirrors. He likes to sit on the floors…propane torch within his reach."
>
> "Nearly his entire diet consists of fruit and juice."
>
> "Crack makes a user anxious and uncomfortable, and trying to relieve the tension, Scott-Heron would sometimes lean to one side or reach one hand across himself to grab his opposite ankle."

> "Monique deLatour, an artist who lived with Scott-Heron for three years [...] says the longest she saw him stay awake was seven days."
>
> "According to deLatour [...] Scott-Heron would sometimes make holes in the walls looking for microphones and cameras. He believed that bad spirits came with crack, and to counteract them he would give money to charities."
>
> "His teeth fell out and he got implants, some of which also fell out – one time when he was onstage in Berlin."
>
> "[Scott-Heron:] 'I'm trying to stay out of traction [...] I feel like I got a piece of gravel up at the top of my spine.' He lit the propane torch and touched the glass tube to his lips. 'Ten to fifteen minutes of this and I don't have pain.'"
>
> "[Scott-Heron:] 'I tried painkillers but after a couple of weeks, I felt like a piece of furniture [...] This I can quit anytime I'm ready.'"
>
> "[Scott-Heron]: 'I have a novel I can write.'" He raised the torch, then paused and said, "'I have everything but the conclusion.'"

The following two quotes, from the same article, are key to what I will take from Scott-Heron's life – in addition to his music, which I'll listen to and carry in my spirit, for the rest of my life.

As Wilkinson shares: "Scott-Heron references people saying he disappeared during the 10 years he spent [in and out of] prison." And,

"Scott-Heron: "'Your life has to consist of more than Black people should unite. You hope they do, but not 24 hours a day.'"

Addiction is a disease Gil Scott-Heron never recovered from; he just barely lived through it. As he shares in "I'm New Here," I think one of the reasons he had no regrets about the hours, days, weeks, years he spent in his Harlem apartment with nothing but his crack/crack pipe to keep him company is because being constantly high out of his mind helped him deal with the deep pain and disappointment of the Revolution not only not being televised, but also witnessing leader after leader either be killed, put in prison, or escape to other countries. I think that like Dr. Martin Luther King Jr., and many other political and/or artist-activists, Gil Scott-Heron had a dream he shared in song after song by articulating racism and oppression over and over in an America where Whiteys on the Moon are far removed from Black folks and their suffering. But unlike Dr. King, Scott-Heron did not have a plan that may have allowed him to recover/regroup, and once all of our leaders were gone and no one new stepped up, he was unable to deal with the fact that instead of uniting, too many Black folks took the "I'm an individual" rather than collective approach. Any chance for the radical change of revolution went up in the crack smoke Gil Scott-Heron disappeared in.

When I heard of his death in 2011, I hadn't thought about Scott-Heron for years. When I looked him up and became aware of his final album, "I'm New Here," I watched a video of Scott-Heron performing it. He looked so old and hollow, old and hollow, old and empty. The sadness in his cracked voice contradicted his insistence that he had no regrets about being on crack for so long. It was like running into a hero on Halloween after midnight – you just know it's a ghost, because he looks too scary to be real. According to Scott-Heron, he only wrote one song on "I'm New Here." It's called "New York is killing me." Scott-Heron also notes that the only reason the album happened is because it was the dream of its producer, Richard Russell. True to Scott-Heron's commitment to the Blues, the first song on it was "Me and the Devil," by the late Blues genius Robert Johnson.

Beginning with my first poem titled "Death," written when I was 13 years old after witnessing a young Black man who'd just been killed by a car, I've written numerous poems to honor people who have passed on to what's next. Gil Scott-Heron has inspired generations of poets (including me), rap artists, and musicians. I end by sharing the free verse sonnet I wrote right after watching "I'm New Here":

Blue Heron Sonnet
For: Gil Scott-Heron

He arrived suddenly like jazz, like a
Bopped Bird song, like love—naked as verse.
Raised between the North and South, at war
with himself and every shade of white pow(d)er.

Tracked truth where it lived in disguise.
Music a Valentine, Black bullets, drums.
Government hatred a constant refrain.
His life a short road map, no rainbows.

Revolution elusive as one love,
hip hop, chance of Black life on white moon.
Sixty-two the number for solitude,
bold face aged too soon, mouth, eyes glisten.

He left yesterday on a Black sunrise.
Took twenty-eight minutes to arrive.

I'm certain Gil Scott-Heron is in a better place. I'm certain he lives with our ancestors, free from pain, free from crack, free.

I wonder why he spent most of his life in New York, if it was killing him?

I wonder if his too-short life would have been different if the Revolution still so needed in this country would have happened in streets filled with the Black people he loved?

Notes

1 Nelson, S. (Director.) (2020). *Crack: Cocain, corruption, & conspiracy*. Netflix.
2 Weems, M. E. (2014). *Blackeyed: Plays and monologues*. Sense Publishers.

9

DREAMSCAPES AND ESCAPEDREAMS: AN AUTOETHNOGRAPHY THROUGH THE ART OF JERRY WEEMS[1]

Bryant Keith Alexander

Art, whether pictorial or performative, invites us into worlds of knowing and being. Whether it is into the mind and world of the artist; into an encounter with nature or states of human experience; reflections of history, race, culture, class and community; or a confrontation with aspects of our own embodied experience, we're forced to either relive, revive, or reimagine spaces of joy, trauma, and the tremulations of lost possibilities and failed promises. Art thus engulfs and propels us into *dreamscapes* – which can be strange, as in the work of Salvador Dali, or at other times can be all too real – and into *escapedreams*: escapes from aspects of everyday living, when we wish we could dream ourselves out of the altogether real.

So with art, we sometimes struggle to interpret meaning, and our complicity in the realism of the known and the unknown. While seemingly individualistic in nature, art also circulates through the *global flows* of culture, media, technology, finance, and the social consciousness of our negotiated realities that often stimulate the autoethnographic impulse in artistic expression.[2] Sometimes, it triggers how we contend with those constructed social presumptions – like justice, equality, democracy, and our presumed dominance over the natural world – for which we are never fully assured of our position. Art helps us to both dream and escape, to critique and resist the everydayness of our being, manifesting as both fantasy and nightmare in a material experience. The work of Los Angeles–based artist Jerry Weems takes me to those places, and then reminds me that I am already there. He creates art as social comment and political intervention – art as a reflective, reflexive, and refractive lens of the everyday.

And with Jerry, art and the experiencing of art is a collaborative spiritual engagement that signals both past and possibility. He tells stories with his paintbrush just as I tell stories with my writing. With paint to canvas and ink to paper, the spiritual

DOI: 10.4324/9781003203520-9

communion is in the viewing and reflecting, the re-coding and remembering of ourselves with and in our cultural past. Each uses cultural symbols as communication and memorial; each uses our critical craft in *spiritual strivings* and *spiritual yearnings*. A collaborative of spirits, we are reunited and made manifest when canvas and words give voice through a visualicity of experience.

I first encountered Weems in May 2007 as he presented a show entitled "Southern Hospitality."[3]

The show consisted of a series of black and white images on masonite board depicting aspects of everyday Black cultural life in the rural South. For me, like Weems, these images in their most simplistic and complex renderings *reanimate in the present the racial civil war they document* as both the enacted violence and the residual effects of difference and indifference to which each reference. In this case, "everyday" is the historicized reality emanating from racial injustice and the manifestations of such origins in the repeated present. Serving as hauntology, the work presents a *temporal and ontological disjunction* that locates us in the past-presence of our racial reality: a specter of our assumed progress.[4]

Each painting offers a narrative in the historiography of the South that resonates with aspects of my own childhood growing up in southwest Louisiana. Living in poverty and rampant racism. Living with a community that still had a line that divided where Blacks lived versus where whites lived. Living with minimally educated Black parents with six other siblings in a two-bedroom house that did not have running water in the kitchen, much less central air or heat. Yet, we persisted. And we thrived.

And while my parents tried to shield their children from the harshness of the still-Jim Crow South, they told stories. They told us their stories, lest we forget the history of the happenings, and to fortify use against the dangers that still existed.

Their stories paralleled Weems' accurate yet sardonic images of *southern hospitality*: a phrase that upholds an "imperialist nostalgia… governing relations of dominance and subordination" as an idealized relational performative of the South.[5]

Joy Ride

Like **"Joy Ride."** My father would tell us *walking while Black stories* about the dangers of leaving the neighborhood, and especially of walking across race lines. He told us about the pleasure that some white folks took in the opportunity to harm young Black boys; he showed us his childhood scars from attacks. Yet, by the time that we were all of age, his physical scars were fading, while the memories continued to flare. We were accruing our own scars to show, both physical and psychological. Our scars are enflamed even more today, as we still engage in the national struggle that "Black Lives Matter": engaged activism on the matter of Black lives, demonstrating that the materiality and humanness of Black people matter in our equal treatment under the law. Still.

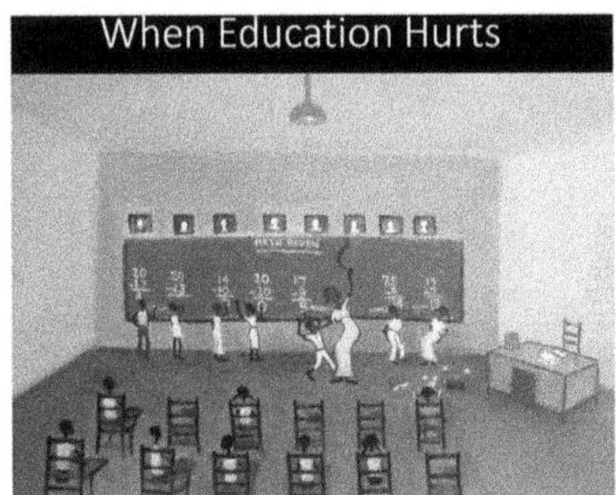
When Education Hurts

Like **"When Education Hurts."** My parents told *mean teacher stories*. Some were white, and would beat Black children for not being responsive to lessons that were incongruent with their cultural knowing. Some were Black teachers who, back in the day, having been enculturated into the racism of schooling through their own training, at times perpetuated pedagogical violence and a performance of their educational credentials against other, younger Black bodies. They punished Black children like my father, who inevitably dropped out of school at the end of fourth grade after being consistently told he was stupid – and with his learning disability never addressed.

Like **"Human Race."** My mother told her two daughters and her five sons *vulnerable Black female stories.* Like the story of when she was attacked, battered, and nearly raped by a group of white boys who were out on a joy ride trolling for Black tail. She was only saved from violation by old Mr. Robinson, who beat the boys off with his cane, which allowed her to get away but left him in the hospital with injuries from which he never fully recovered.

Like **"Miscegenation."** They told *one drop rule stories* that depicted the complicated histories of race relations in southwest Louisiana with the persistence of the "one Drop Rule," which not only made determinations of race but produced shades of difference. The politics of skin color and histories of miscegenation, both intended and unavoidable, established a pernicious racism of skin color, hair texture, and facial and bodily features even within the Black community. The result is a performed propriety of privilege still prevalent in many parts of the South.

Like **"Chopping Cotton"** and **"Picking Cotton."** Both represented continued forms of slave labor through indentured servitude, or peonage. *Also called debt slavery or debt servitude, peonage is a system where an employer compels a worker to pay off a debt with work. Legally, peonage was outlawed by Congress in 1867.* Yet, the Vagrancy Act of 1866 *forced into employment, for terms of up to the three months, any person who appeared to be unemployed or homeless – intentionally ensnaring the hundreds of thousands of newly free "African-Americans" from slavery.* The law itself was in force until 1904,[6] but we know that in the South, peonage and the practices of vagrancy penalties lingered long after – until the near-present.[7]

My mother told *daughter of a sharecropper stories* about the only type of work her father could get after returning from military service. Working as a sharecropper came with a set of living conditions that was offered just enough for him to feed his family, but not enough to prosper in any other way. My mother described it as grueling seasonal work with a long history of disparity between the rights, benefits, and privileges of the landowner versus those who worked the land. The system was held in place by governmental law and racial rule, which were one and the same.

Like **"Home Coming."** I further contribute my own stories through my parents' and family's investment in my education. I return home ritually to stay culturally and communally connected. It is an act done out of love and as a defense against their fear, which is the fear of many parents of color with first-generation college students. They fear their child will learn so much and become so achieved in their intellect that they will forget about family, friends, and culture – and what *they* taught you. They fear their child will no longer respect them, after they have surpassed them in education. Some fear their child will become *whitewashed* in the multiple and varied interpretations of that phrase. They fear their child will be ashamed of where they come from. They fear their child will not come home again – and not recognize their role in family and community.

Yet despite their fears, they love and support the dreams of their children so much that they send them away as a personal sacrifice for their own possibility.[8] These were the fears and hopes that my mother whispered in my ear every time I left home – and every time I delayed my return.

And like **"Church Sunday."** Religion as the cornerstone of many Black communities. My parents told and lived *stories of the communal rituals of faith* through religion, celebrating survival with the hope of transcendence from the daily woes of everyday Black life in the South. I was raised in a Catholic family. I was an altar boy, cantor, choir member, usher, and now a Eucharistic Minister. And like my father, I was on my way to becoming a Knight of St. Peter Claver, a Black men's service group honoring the life of Jesuit Priest St. Peter Claver. Currently a Dean at a Catholic-Jesuit university, I may still become a knight to honor my father. I still go to church as ritual practice. And I put myself on my knees every day as an act of prayer; as an act of humility; and as a continual act of locating the body in relation to the ground, in relation to the dust to which this mortal body will most certainly return to be symbolically reintegrated with nature, and the ancestors.

My fixation with this collection by Jerry Weems works in/as a realization that I am engaging in *the labor of contemplating*, and not only how I believe the artist intended his audience to engage with this collection. I have in fact entered and/or reentered the worlds that are depicted in the paintings, and the scenes that we both share and claim and (re)member ourselves to.[9]

I believe that the paintings force an audiencing stance that requires the one viewing the painting to either actively project or intuit themselves in relation to the depicted scenes – as protagonist, antagonist, or empowered social being. The faceless images of both Blacks and whites in the paintings allow such a projection without displacing the particularity of embodied experiences. As Elyse Pineau might suggest, I am experiencing "a determinacy of art and witness fused together in the act of attending," and now in the act of sharing the experience of attending.[10] In the process, the artist and I also engage in our shared intimacy as Black *men of a certain age* from the South, with the life and psychological imprints of our specific racial and culturally located geographical upbringing.

But there are three pieces of this collection that I literally *live with*, and see and study every day, as I sit at the desk in my home office.

The original pieces **"Twin Towers,"** "**Chain Gain,"** and "**Let the Good Times Roll**" are situated in my direct view. They press against my daily vision, my senses, and my sensibilities in my home office. They serve as *dreamscapes and escapedreams*: as landscapes or scenes with a strangeness or mysterious characteristic of dreams or nightmares, the depicted images both painfully and joyfully familiar. I purchased them from the artist and keep them as a juxtaposition of realities and possibilities of Black cultural life, especially in relation to the particularity of my own Black male existence and persistence in a country in which we must continually profess that "Black Lives Matter."

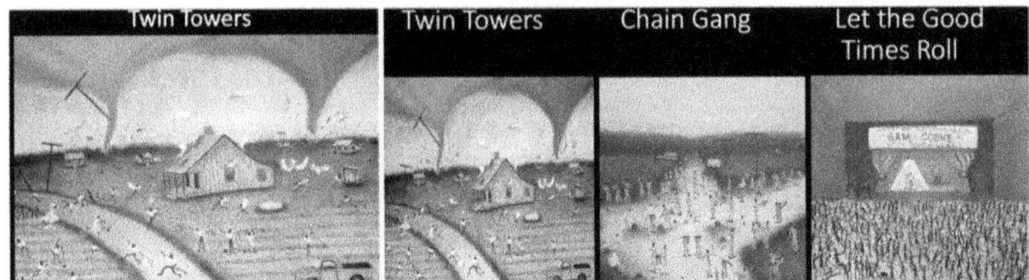

The first piece, "Twin Towers" is situated behind my back when I am sitting at my desk. It is a reminder of my past growing up in southwest Louisiana in relation to my current location of Los Angeles. It is a past for me, but to some degree it is a current relative of my siblings, who are still living in our hometown.

I think of it in relation to the destruction of Hurricane Katrina, along with a series of devastating weather formations that ritually threaten and decimate property and lives. I keep it as a reminder that *there but for the grace of God go I.*

The second, **"Chain Gang"** is situated on a far wall from my desk. It keeps me up at night, along with the continual nightly news reels of violence against Black people in the form of public murders and beatings at protests.

#Ferguson
#Blacklivesmatter
#icantbreathe
#HandsUpDon'tShoot
#sayhername
#BriannaTaylor
#TrayvonMartin
#GeorgeFloyd
#PhilandoCastile
#AltonSterling
#MichaelBrown
#TanishaAnderson
#DanielPiude
#AtatianaJefferson
#Aura Rosser
#StephonClark
#BothamJean
#MicheleCusseaux
#FreddieGray
#Taniesha Fonville
#Eric Garndner
#AkaiGurley

#GabriellaNevarez
#TamirRice
#RashardBrooks
too-many-goddam-hastags-for-murdered-black-people-at-the-hands-of-unregulated-police.[11]

The image of "Chain Gang" also brings me to tears because when I am home visiting Louisiana, I can see this scene still playing out on the highways and byways. They are instances in which cheap, imprisoned Black male labor is carried out in institutionally marked and dehumanizing uniforms, Black and white stripes or blaze orange, as the men clean ditches and roadsides under the watchful eyes of armed guards. The image speaks to me: *there but for the grace of God go I*, with the knowledge that two of my five biological brothers and two of my nephews have served time in the Louisiana penal system. My life stands in/as juxtaposition to theirs. The differences or vast, but the potential for conflating our Black male bodies is always too close.

So, when I write, *there but for the grace of God go I*, this is not about constructing an escape narrative. I am not immune to the everyday violence against Black bodies, no matter where and how this Black body is positioned. My current *class situation* as a professor and academic dean does not make me invisible as I walk the highways and byways of everyday living. My Black boojee-ass does not pass for anything but just another Black man living and dying in America.

Yet, the other image I keep close to me – closest to me, to my immediate left, within touching distance as I sit at my home desk – gives me complete joy. **"Let the Good Times Roll."**

The painting depicts a scene of dancing at a Sam Cooke concert, probably in the late 1950s or early 1960s, before Cooke's death at age 34 in 1964 in Los Angeles. The picture features for me the breadth and depth of African American expressive culture: musicality, dancing, singing, clothing and style, walking, strolling, joking, and juking. It depicts the creative use of singing and dancing as literal, spiritual, and rhetorical soul raising; as direct and indirect discourse, as proclamation and subversion; as a celebration anointing a moment, as well as a transcendence of space and time.[12] And because Cooke was a son of Clarksdale, Mississippi, the joyfulness is also a celebration of Black excellence and pride.

I see myself throughout this image. I am a traveling character. One time, I am the male character in the bottom left-hand corner of the image doing a splits on the floor. At another time, I am a character in the middle of the crowd engaged in polyrhythmic motions with a bent, grounded body and strategically thrusting movements that are African in a nature yet influenced by the gestures of local culture.

Look at the picture closely, and you can see the animation of activity come alive in the painting.

These are the images, the counternarratives and realities that I carry of Black cultural life and of Black people of the South. This is the image that serves not just as juxtaposition to "Chain Gang," but as antidote to it.

This is the dreamscape that I also experience every time I go back home to Louisiana when my younger sister takes me to the local Black clubs: *The Willow Lounge, The Miami Moon,* a place called *"Grown Folks,"* and others. These are places where Black folks are dancing up a storm dressed in the finery of their own fashion, with bodies moving bodies to the rhythms of music. Here is a freedom of expression and joy that brings me to tears – every time. Maybe it is in this scene of "Let the Good Times Roll" that there is a "mapping of hope and effect,"[13] not completely unlike the collection at large. *There in the grace of God go I.*

It is in these paintings that I can further see Black subjectivity defining itself in relation to community. Here, we witness the emergent possibilities that come from shared experience in times of tragedy and struggle – along with collective celebration in times of joy and worship – interweaving the everydayness of Black southern life during the period depicted in the paintings – and now.[14] Thus, the work of Jerry Weems, for me, activates a material experience: *a materiality of experience* that penetrates beyond the sensibility of just viewing art, to establish a fundamental relationship between viewer and object of art in material form.

Such form manifests as a product of effort – a technology of doing and a passion that is physically created by the artist and becomes bodily felt through engagement with the art. Intimacy with the image is established through my eyes when I see, and through my fingertips when I trail them along the bumpy details of the surface. It enters my blood and goes straight to my mind and heart through the nerve endings of an experiencing body with the materiality of art. Thus, the work creates a complicity of blood, remembrance, and activism with the artist that becomes corporeal.[15] I find myself altogether pulled into the world of the art, both painfully and happily situated on each canvas. Each canvas is a testimony to the possibilities of living, surviving, and thriving while Black in America. And as Sam Cooke sang, *"There have been times that I thought I couldn't last for long. But now I think I'm able to carry on, It's been a long, a long time coming, But I know a change is gonna come, oh yes it will."*[16]

Notes

1 This performative essay is based on: Chapter 2, Southern Hospitality Indeed!: A Performative Engagement with Art Depictions of African American Culture in the Rural South. In Alexander, B.K. (2012). *The performative sustainability of race: Reflections on black culture and the politics of identity* (pp. 53–83). Peter Lang Press.

2 See Appadurai, A. (1990). Disjunctive and difference in the global cultural economy. *Theory Culture Society*, 7, 295; Cheprasov, A. (2020, October 16). The five dimensions of global cultural flow. Study.com. https://study.com/academy/lesson/the-five-dimensions-of-global-cultural-flow.html. For materials on arts-based approaches to autoethnography, see Ownby, T. (2013). Critical visual methodology: Photographs and narrative text as a visual autoethnography. *Online Journal of Communication and Media Technologies*; Chaplin, E. (2011). The photo diary as an autoethnographic method. In E. Margolis & L. Pauwels (Eds.), *The SAGE handbook of visual research methods*. SAGE. https://dx.doi.org/10.4135/9781446268278.n13; Suominen, A. (2003). *Writing with photographs, re-constructing self: And art-based autoethnographic inquiry*. Dissertation, Ohio State University; Ellis, C. (2003). Art as autoethnography/

Autoethnography as art. *The ethnographic I: A methodological novel about autoethnography* (pp. 184–192). AltaMira Press.

3 Jerry Weems presented the show as a part of his MFA thesis in the Art Department at California State University Los Angeles. The author thanks him for giving his permission to use the images in this book.

4 See Derrida, J. (1994). *Specters of Marx: The state of the debt, the work of mourning and the new international.* (P. Kamuf, Trans.). Routledge; Hauntology. in *Wikipedia.* https://en.wikipedia.org/wiki/Hauntology.

5 McPherson, T. (2003). *Reconstructing Dixie: Race, gender, and nostalgia in the imagined south* (p. 9). Duke University Press. McPherson is referencing hooks, b. (1992). *Black looks: Race and representation* (p. 173). South End Press. hooks quotes Rosaldo, R. (1989). *Culture and truth: The remaking of social analysis.* Beacon Press.

6 For more on the relationship between slavery and peonage, see PBS. Slavery v. Peonage. https://www.pbs.org/tpt/slavery-by-another-name/themes/peonage/.

7 I use this construction to describe another piece of art by Jerry Weems entitled, "Victims of Peonage and Vagrancy Laws." The painting, not included in this essay, appears as the cover for the book Alexander. B. K., & Weems, M. E. (2021). *Still hanging: Performance texts deconstructing racism.* Brill | Sense Publishing. The art will also be included in a future book chapter further *exploring the worlds created and reimagined in the art of Jerry E. Weems.*

8 I used the construction of these fears experienced by the parents of First Generation college students in a keynote address entitled "A welcome, a warning and a wish: On entering LMU through the 'First to Go Program' in the Year 2020" for the 10th Anniversary Cohort of the *First to Go Program* at Loyola Marymount University (August, 2020).

9 Madison, D. S. (2011). The labor of reflexivity. *Cultural Studies ⟷ Critical Methodologies, 1*(2),129.

10 Pineau, E. (2011). Intimacy, empathy, activism: A performative engagement with children's wartime art. In N. K. Denzin & M. D. Giardina (Eds.), *Qualitative inquiry and global crisis* (p. 208). Left Coast Press.

11 Chughtai, A. (n.d.). Know their names: Black people killed by police in the U.S. Al Jazeera. https://interactive.aljazeera.com/aje/2020/know-their-names/index.html.

12 See White, S., & White, G. (1998). *Stylin: African American expressive culture: From its beginning to the Zoot suit.* Cornell University Press.

13 Muñoz, J. E. (2006). Stages: Queers, punks, and the utopian performative. In S. D. Madison & J. Hamera (Eds.), *The SAGE handbook of performance studies* (p. 19). SAGE.

14 Here, I am alluding to how Kimberly Brown furthers an argument against a "coherent, consistent, and complete 'identity' for Black women" in favor for a more dynamic identity that is self-determining and emerges in relation to shifting audiences. Brown, K. N. (2010). *Writing the Black Revolutionary Diva: Women's subjectivity and the decolonizing text* (pp. 61–62). Indiana University Press.

15 I discovered the important work of Christiana Murdoch Mills when I was under deadline to submit the essay. I will be revisiting this work in greater detail for future related projects. See Mills, C. N. (2009). Materiality as the basis for the aesthetic experience in contemporary art. Graduate Student Theses, Dissertations, & Professional Papers https://scholarworks.umt.edu/etd/1289. Here I must also note the important critical analysis of Nina Lozano on *new materialism* and *border materialism.* Lozano establishes "a theoretical framework that offers scholars a lens to examine how

object-oriented things and matter intersect with bodies… rooted in neoliberal economic structures within specific geographical boundaries mediated by human agency for political change." Lozano, M. N. (2019). *Not one more! Feminicido on the border.* The Ohio State University Press. Quote from public presentation given by Lozano on October 13, 2020, Faculty Pub Night, Hannon Library, Loyola Marymount University.

16 Cooke, S. (1954). A change is gonna come. *National Archives.* https://www.archives.gov/exhibits/documented-rights/exhibit/section4/detail/change-is-gonna-come-lyrics.html.

SECTION II
Introduction to Resistance

Bryant Keith Alexander and Mary E. Weems

Up until this point in the book, we have already used the words "resist," "resisting," or "resistance" at least 20 times – maybe you can find them. Maybe you can find them written in poetic and performative language, spoken in relation to our response to terrorism, and in relation to hope and rage. Maybe, you can find them in terms of resisting stories, Blackness as an ontology of resistance, resistance and critique of/to Donald Trump, the crafted resistance to capitalistic bloat, and the notion of embodying an artistic rage of resistance. They represent resistance as public protest against the killing of unarmed Black people; dancing as resistance by gay folks living on the pulse; and the Black performance of resistance in the everyday religiosity of faith.

Maybe you can find those references to resistance that precede this section, knowing that resistance is laced throughout this project and beyond this section. **What is resistance to you?** Is it a refusal to accept or comply with something; the attempt to prevent something by action or argument; or the ability not to be affected by something, especially adversity? **What do you resist? How do you perform resistance?** Is it a performance of resistance to emergent attacks or encroachments on your comfort zones, on your mobility, on your freedom or economic status? **Do you resist this, but not that?** Or is it an ongoing enactment of resistance to social structures that impact your daily being because of some dense particularity that makes you *you*, be it race, sex, gender, sexuality, age, country of origin, body type, able bodiedness, and its presumed opposite?

If you can't immediately answer these questions, think again. If you cannot answer these questions, then think about those of us – your friends and colleagues, or the marked others in your life who are consistently resisting the fact that they have been marked as "other" to your sense of self, or to your sense of being

DOI: 10.4324/9781003203520-102

in the majority to their marginalized designations. Think about we who answer these questions quickly and consistently.

What cultural capital due you use that validates your special status? What cultural capitol do you storm *capitol do you storm* to protect your privilege to be privileged in the places you call home? In what country do you live? Maybe, like the United States of America, that bastion of democracy, yours still struggles to define the terms of diversity, equity, and inclusion. Along with the guaranteeing the rights of all citizens, what are the struggles for some in marking the difference between activism and protest marches, versus insurrection, sedition, or treason? **What do you resist and how do you enact a performance of resistance? For change? Or to retain your status of privilege and control?**

And then, separately from the "what" of these questions**, let us ask: Why do you resist?** Do you resist because of the immediate present? Or do you resist because of the lessons taught by history and learned from history?

We, Mary and I, are sincerely asking you to locate yourself in resistance. Where is the "I" in resistance that stands for you? Locate it; then critique it. The answers to many of these questions speak to "why black folk [are] full of dangerous dreaming… and resistive revisions." Moreover, "The act of conceiving of an alternative world, a racial utopia, [is] a gesture of radical resistance that interrupt[s] the totalizing force of white supremacy"[1] and frees the Black spirit.

What does your spirit resist? And what resistance do you perform for the sake of your spirit?

10

UNPRECEDENTED TIMES (JANUARY 6, 2021), OR: THE INSURRECTION WAS TELEVISED AND NEW NORMAL (JANUARY 6, 2021)

Bryant Keith Alexander

Unprecedented Times (January 6, 2021), Or: The Insurrection Was Televised

That phrase has been used repeatedly of late.

Of late, like during *Trump-Times* and *Covid-Times* which are almost indistinguishable relative to pain, suffering, social distancing, restrictive migration, discriminative threat, rampant death, and coordinated civil insurrection.

Times in which the very face of how decisions are made in this country under force, coercion, manipulation, threat, and bullying are being illuminated.

Times in which the far-right Republican ideologies of a corrupt racist *dishonest president*[2] have turned back the clock on the standards of human sociality across these United States of America – advocating white supremacist actions, advocating anarchy, advocating voter fraud and suppression, and advocating racism *from the seat of the White House*.

Times in which long-standing relationships characterized by modeling democracy, cooperation, and conciliation with countries around the world have been compromised by the leadership of the 45th President of these United States of America. *The world is watching*.

Times in which the world heard a United States presidential candidate boast about grabbing women "by the pussy" on national television – along with stories of Trump's disregard and disrespect for women in both the private and public domain that emerged without consequence to his eventual election – and when a post-election degradation of human social relations across boundaries of sex, sexuality, gender, national origin, race relations, and national security became our national disgrace.[3]

Times in which a sitting US president showed blind disregard for the growing danger of coronavirus and ignored recommended precautions, while hundreds of thousands[4] of Americans died – and continue to die – with a disproportioned number of deaths by people of color and the poor. The disregard continued until

DOI: 10.4324/9781003203520-10

the president himself contracted COVID-19, and even then, the toxicity of his biological system and psychological make-up proved more viral than the virus.

Times when threats and actions are persistently perpetuated by a sitting US president – contradicting every principle on which this country stands – in an attempt to persecute immigrants: separating parents from minor children, holding unaccompanied minors in detention camps, seeking to overturn the legality of DACA (Deferred Action for Childhood Arrivals) programs, and threatening to build a wall between the United States and Mexico to prevent families from seeking a better life.[5]

Times when a sitting U.S. president sought to retract, restrict, and restrain the conditions under which LGBTQ+ individuals could serve in their country's military.[6]

Times when the United States is experiencing a dramatic resurgence of overt violence and killing of Black men and women in the dailiness of our habits and habitus at the hands of police officers sworn to serve and protect, along with a rise of white supremacist actions that are constructed as performances of Americanism.

I am writing on January 6, 2021, and live coverage is happening on every national news channel in the nation, as the United States Capitol in Washington, D.C., has been over-taken by Trump supporters trying to halt democracy during the confirmation of the presidential election. I'm watching an attack on democracy that was overtly called for, incited by, sanctioned by, and lead by a sitting president to both exercise his power over right-wing groups – i.e., QANON, Proud Boys, and MAGA – and to continue his reign of white terror on this country. He incited the protestors to infiltrate democratic processes then sat back, Tweeted, and fueled the fire he started. He was summarily blocked from both Twitter and Facebook.[7] A sitting, although resistantly exiting, US president!

> White protestors who stormed the U.S. Capitol and engaged in looting, violence, insurrection, and vandalism.
>
> White protestors who engaged in acts of sedition against democracy, and against the progress of diversity, equity and inclusion initiatives.
>
> White protestors who have activated violence with guns, with at least five related deaths at the time of this writing in and around the United States Capitol building.
>
> White protestors who made necessary the deployment of the U.S. armed National Guard and the FBI – ordered by the vice president, not the president – to restore order within and outside of the United States capital.
>
> White protestors who engaged in overt lawlessness, waiving every variation of confederate, Marxist, and white supremacist flag *with pride.*
>
> White protestors who were supported and incited not only by the sitting (although resistantly exiting) United States President, but by sitting and incoming white Republican Congress members and staff.

> White protestors who, according to some reports, targeted both new and returning Black members of Congress and their staff, moving from "ballots to bullets" as resistance to democracy.
>
> White protestors who benefited from a "tremendous and total law enforcement failure that occurred today" that is suspicious considering the event that was planned and executed.[8] This mass maylay/melee and the reality that these protestors were able to infiltrate the United States Capitol is neither accidental nor a failure of the system of military policing. Just substitute the white racists for Black Lives Matters protestors, and you would witness different outcomes, regulations, and disciplinary actions on Black bodies.
>
> These *domestic terrorists* with guns drawn fired on the House floor of the United States Capitol in an overt act of treason, signaling a breach in American democracy and showing their stronghold on racism and hate in America.

The insurrection (not the revolution*) was televised that day*! The insurrection of white folks behaving badly to maintain their sense of white power and control in these United States of America was televised and memorialized as a testament to white rage, and the privilege to perform it on an international scale.

I am sitting here with a large screen television in the background thinking → This is unprecedented? NO!

This is the face of racism that most African-Americans encounter every day, overtly and covertly. This is the implicit bias of our critical academic and psychological discourses made explicit to reveal, in turn, the social, political, and racial animus that is always at play in America.[9] They were not defending democracy. They were defending the superiority of the white psyche to which Trump validates and promotes in a false claim to Make America Great Again.

Whether this matter is resolved with prosecutions and convictions for all involved in the paramilitary coup, including our 45th United States president, will speak to the future of democracy in this country. *Black Lives Matter.*

Postscript: Two weeks later, same location: January 20, 2021. Joseph R. Biden is inaugurated at the 46th President of the United States of America, and Kamala Harris is inducted as the first woman, and the first woman of African-American and Asian decent, to serve as the Vice President of the United States of America.

Quoting Biden: "Every disagreement doesn't have to become a cause for war… the Dream of justice will be deferred no longer… democracy has prevailed… God bless America."

New Normal (January 6, 2021)

That phrase has been used repeatedly of late. It refers to a seemingly bizarre situation, recognizably abnormal, that one needs to get used to as the ongoing – and thus the new, regular – state of things. *The new normal.*

But I have always resisted the "old normal."

The "old normal" that perpetuated and permitted overt racism in America.

The "old normal" that did not recognize the human dignity of the huddled masses longing to be free despite what that big white lady in the New York harbor professed.

The "old normal" that has maintained a caste system of white supremacy and Black degradation as an historic economic model.[10]

The "old normal" that left scars on the backs of Big Joe and Big Bertha – scars of slavery so deep that they inadvertently passed them along on the bodies of their progeny, along with faith, persistence, tenacity, and true grit flowing through our blood.

The "old normal" that plays out on the streets of everyday life – and even in the Ivory Tower, where liberal minds supposedly prevail, and where rhetorics of implicit bias linger with a stench on the breath of some who approach cries for DEI with strategies of containment, like hush money for histories of exclusion.

The "old normal" in which "Black grief is perceived as threat and white rage is treated as sacrament."[11]

The "old normal" that still calls into question the Black queer as a double damnation in humanity.

The "old normal" that stands as our collective history, where words and practices like inequity were forged in steel as a natural order, but not in God's kingdom.

I, too, yearn for a new normal. But not just one that is regulated by our newfound appreciation for technology through a coronavirus informed exodus. Not one made determinative in the residues of a corrupt commander-in-chief whose 45th status will live in infamy. Not one situated in the aftermath of living through the traumas of our times; one that emerges from the ashes like a phoenix with a newfound resistance and renewal of hope.

"I, too" yearn for a new (new) normal that demonstrates for equality through my persevering patriotism: for the potentiality of Americanism, for the Black person, and for all people of color, across cosmologies and gendered possibilities. *I, too* sing for a new America that will realize the covenant that all men, women, and particular others are created equal.

We have not yet seen the "new normal," but like the second coming of Jesus, I hope that we will not just recognize him when he comes, but we will plan for his arrival and the renewal of possibility

I stand poised for what is to come from this terrible time – poised for *a new (new) normal.*

Notes

1 Dyson, M.E. (2004). *The Michael Eric Dyson reader* (pp. 480–481). Basic Civitas.

2 Davan Maharaj and Nicholas Goldberg (introduction). *Our dishonest president: The Los Angeles Times Editorial Board.* Berkeley, CA: Heyday.

3 Fahrenthold, D. A. (2016). Trump recorded having extremely lewd conversation about women in 2005. *Washington Post.*www.washingtonpost.com/politics/trump-recorded-having-extremely-lewd-conversation-about-women-in-2005/2016/10/

07/3b9ce776-8cb4-11e6-bf8a-3d26847eeed4_story.html; Berensen, T. (2016). Donald Trump personally attacked the women accusing him of sexual assault' *Time*, October 14. https://time.com/4531872/donald-trump-sexual-assault-accusers-attack/. Also see: Goins, M. N., McAlister, J. & Alexander, B. K. (2020). *The Routledge handbook of gender and communication.* Routledge.

4 See DACA: https://www.supremecourt.gov/opinions/19pdf/18-587_5ifl.pdf.

5 See Jackson, H. & Kube, C. (n.d.). *Trump's controversial transgender military policy goes into effect.* https://www.nbcnews.com/feature/nbc-out/trump-s-controversial-transgender-military-policy-goes-effect-n993826

6 "Facebook and Twitter lock Trump's accounts after posting video praising rioters: The video showed Trump repeating unfounded claims that the election was taken from him and encouraging his supporters to disperse after violence erupted at the Capitol." https://www.nbcnews.com/tech/social-media/facebook-youtube-twitter-remove-video-trump-amid-chaos-capitol-n1253157.

7 MSNBC Live, Rachel Maddow interviewing (1/13/2021).

8 See Van Jones, CNN https://www.youtube.com/watch?v=JLBLgH3PAeI.

9 Isabel Wilkerson (2020). *Caste: The origins of our discontents.* New York: Random House.

10 Tweet from Rev. Jacqui Lewis, Ph.D., January 6, 2021.

11 "I, Too." Langston Hughes https://www.poetryfoundation.org/poems/47558/i-too.

11

CULTURAL CAPITA(O)L

Mary E. Weems

> *According to French sociologist Pierre Bourdieu, who coined the term in a 1973 paper titled "Cultural Reproduction and Social Reproduction," cultural capital is: "The accumulation of knowledge, behaviors, and skills that a person can tap into to demonstrate one's* ***cultural*** *[read: 'white cultural'] competence and social status."*[1]

January 6, 2021

Question: What is behind the MASSIVE Security failure at the Capitol today, January 6, 2021?

Answer: In part, Donald Trump's failure to issue an order to the National Guard to prepare for an insurrection he'd consistently been signaling his base to execute, resulting in what's supposed to be the best security force in the country being totally unprepared for the riot that ensued.

The first feeling that washed over my mind, body, and spirit like frigid Atlantic Ocean water was the stark, obvious, and overwhelming difference between the way these approximately 100,000 white rioters were being treated as compared to Black people anywhere in this country who engage in their right to peaceful protest, which, during the T-rump administration, has been singularly focused on rampant police violence against innocent-until-proven-guilty Black men and women. Think Eric Garner, Atatiana Jefferson, George Floyd, etc. The list is long and continuing. Most recently, in Kenosha, Wisconsin, the District Attorney refused to bring charges against the police officer who shot Jacob Blake in the back seven times as he reached into the back seat of his car, noting the he (the white District Attorney) had never been afraid of the police.

DOI: 10.4324/9781003203520-11

The words of James Baldwin and Michelle Alexander are instructive here:

> The truth is that this country does not know what to do with its [B]lack population now that the [B]lacks are no longer a source of wealth, are no longer to be bought and sold and bred, like cattle; and they especially do not know what to do with young [B]lack men who pose as devastating a threat to the economy as they do to the morals of young white cheerleaders. It is not at all accidental that the jails and the army and the needle claim so many, but there are still too many prancing around for the public comfort.[2]

> "The United States now has the highest rate of incarceration in the world."[3]

> "In some states, [B]lack men have been admitted to prison on drug* charges at rates twenty to fifty times greater than those of white men."[4]
> **Note that many of them are doing time for selling marijuana, which is now legal at least to some degree in many states including Ohio.*

The 401-year history of Black people in this country has always included elements of terror, trauma, and tragedy. Beginning with slavery, the Civil War – which is still taught as having been fought to free the "slaves," but was always about stopping the South from seceding from the Union – then Reconstruction, and its brief attempt to do the right thing by Black folks (resulting in the beginning of the Ku Klux Klan), followed by renewed efforts to oppress Black people in every way possible, including Convict Leasing, which criminalized anything a Black man/woman did, such as standing on the street without having a job. The Convict Leasing run by former slave owners was supported by law enforcement and several U.S. presidents. It continued the free labor that helped lay the financial foundation for many of the country's major businesses, aided and abetted by Jim Crow laws, segregation, and other stated and unstated policies designed to not only keep Black people oppressed, but also to ensure they'd never fully enjoy the fruits of their labor, guaranteeing that white privilege would always dictate who would control and mostly benefit from all aspects of the hierarchy of an American society founded on the idea of being class-less and equal. According to the film "Slavery by Another Name," the tragedy of Convict Leasing didn't end until just before the start of World War II, when a white man caught up in the madness was killed. There was a sudden outcry to dismantle the unjust system which had resulted in the brutalizing and deaths of hundreds of Black men and some Black women.

As Baldwin alludes to in the above quote, the truth is that Black slaves comprised the number one asset of white folks for centuries. Once that period was over, white racists have done everything under the sun, moon, and stars to exploit us and keep us on the bottom – including limiting our employment options; rioting against school desegregation and then immediately working to de facto re-segregate;

imposing mass incarceration; changing welfare laws to eliminate the presence of the Black father in the home; and manipulating affirmative action laws to deny Black people the benefits it was designed, in part, to provide. For example, employers now make certain to interview Black people for the position, but then hire white applicants, all the while quietly claiming that the main recipients of its benefits are Black people when it's *always* been white women.

Whiteness has always been the most important cultural capital in this country, while Black culture has always been simultaneously commodified and devalued – a cruel paradox which continues today. The situation is implicitly justified by the gist of Moynihan's 1965 Report, which supported the notion of Blacks living within a culture of poverty.[5] The Report cited slavery as the reason for the dismantling of the Black family, exacerbated by high unemployment among Black men, and posited that households headed by Black women had resulted in a culture of poverty. The irony of a white man, who at the time was the assistant secretary of the Department of Labor, blaming Black people for a system put in place by white folks to keep them in their so-called "place," coupled with its long-term residual effects – including President Lyndon Johnson's War on Poverty – ignores the fact that there have always been white broken homes and white poverty, which has always been virtually ignored in favor of keeping a laser focus on Black people.

This Evolution will not be Televised

One million poems, and blood

paintings pressed between fingers

not leaving prints

Picasso and the brotha from another planet

passing each other on a New York street,

the brotha pullin' his coat, Picasso

opening his trench to reveal his wares

hanging from the lining like cheap,

imitation watches

Meanwhile, watching the fun ghosts

smoking huge dollar bills walk

down fast streets stepping on all

the cracks

Mothers create dance in large kitchens

with wooden floors, the mistress
of the house sits in the pantry quietly
taking notes
Contrary to popular belief Claude McKay's
tombstone does not say "fuck all you mothafuckas"
and James Brown was the Godfather of soul
before time started
Starting to looking around can hurt if you Black
and wonder why everybody carries
copies of your work in back pockets
while your paint brushes rest in jelly jars,
you canvas shop in the backs of grocery stores
days food is delivered
Basquiat and Hendrix took a long trip
all their baggage was pawned the day
after they left
George Carlin said white folks should never,
ever play the blues their job is to give the blues
to Blacks
Our image, our braids, our music, our mistakes,
our asses, our rhythms are played on TV
like a long 78 album in commercial after commercial
This is a never-ending story that won't be televised
But:
Baraka already wrote a poem about it
Miles played it on the way to the grave
Zora copied the story 100 times
Toni Morrison keeps trying to change the ending
In the end, Alex Haley's Roots were sold

old artists look for their fortunes in fertile palms,
lose the ability to count their blessings
on Sunday
Seems like Lena sang "Stormy Weather" once
and the sky got stuck
Which reminds me: What is the present value of 1
Billion dreams slit, sucked, scarred, riffed,
ripped?
B.B. King stopped lovin' having the blues years ago
kept playing as a reminder
This is a never-ending story
an evolution
that will not be televised
P.S. Back on the Block the brotha from another planet
watches Picasso sketch graffiti in the subway.[6]

When it comes to politics, timing is everything. Something that's not being stated enough in our current chaos is why Donald J. T-rump, a barely educated, racist, sexist, misogynist, xenophobic failure at everything he's ever attempted with the singular exception of television show host was elected president in the first place: blatant racism and fear stoked by T-rump and felt by the millions who voted him into office, including the tens of thousands who stormed the Capitol today.

Nomination

Tuesday, June 3, 2008
James Brown DJs in Heaven, his splits deeper, he screams
love talk. All around him the party's
up there – Phyllis Wheatley boogaloos
with DuBois, King prays for the brother, Malcolm
grins and writes, 3 of the Temps, Marvin Gaye and Miles Davis
line up for a midnight concert.
America wakes up early. In one-hour Champagne

and Rose sellout in the hood, rural towns,
the burbs where signs on doors mark places
Obama's the guest who's coming to dinner.
All bookies off pay, for once smiling
as money leaves their pockets faster
than winners can say Barack Hussein
Obama. People hug, high-five, holla,
Give dap. Children dream of being
old enough to vote.
Shout-outs hesitate for a moment.
We who've lived long enough to lose
heroes, continue constant prayers. It's not
hate we're afraid of, it's what hate can do
to a moment.[7]

As soon as Barack Hussein Obama was elected as the first Black president in November 2008, there was a dramatic increase in hate groups, hate crimes, and violence against Blacks, Jews, Muslims, and the LGBTQ community, including the Pulse Tragedy. Black men in particular began to be shot and killed by police at a rate so fast that before we could finish mourning the murder of one Black man (and to a lesser degree women), another one was being reported in the news. Obama was depicted as a monkey, the White House lawn decorated with watermelons, Michelle Obama was referred to as the ugliest First Lady in the history of the country, and so on.

Bottom line, with the help of white racists ranging from those with even a modicum of power, like David Duke, to presidential power, like Donald J. T-Rump, hate became as popular as baseball, and disinformed white folks became terrified they were going to have to share their privilege/power with Black people. Make no mistake, this race hatred and fear is mainly responsible for our shifting from the Information Age to the Dis-Information Age, for the 74 million-plus people who voted for T-rump in 2020 (9% Black), for the debacle I witnessed today watching thousands of white people attack the Capitol, waving Don't Tread on Me, Confederate, American, and Trump 2020 flags, many scaling its walls like mountain climbers and rushing police who did absolutely "nothing" to stop them. In fact, reportedly several police were seen posing with the rioters for pictures and encouraging them to keep up the good work. One woman who was interviewed after being exposed to tear gas was asked "what" they were doing, and she responded, "This is a revolution." I watched as white folks broke out windows, smashed through doors, put MAGA hats on statues, and took pictures posing beside them. I watched as white folks stormed the Senate during the important work of certifying the electoral vote required to officially begin the peaceful transfer of power to Joe Biden and Kamala Harris. I watched as our elected politicians cowered between rows, escaping to safe spaces. I watched as one white man put his feet up on Speaker Nancy Pelosi's desk, heard later that her computer was stolen. Five people lost their lives during the insurrection, including one white woman and an injured Capitol Hill police officer who died in the hospital.

The difference between the treatment of white folks breaking the law and terrorizing elected officials and Black folks righteously assembling to protest the unjust killing of Black people is unavoidable, and so obvious no one with two eyes and a mind can deny it. It highlights, with the terrible clarity of a magnifying glass left in the sun, that in the United or Un-tied States of America, white privilege is the only cultural capita(o)l that matters, even when in the process of attacking our democracy and everything it is supposed to represent.

Acknowledged or not, we are in the midst of a double pandemic: the health-related one caused by a new virus which makes the body physically sick and is sometimes deadly (especially for Black folks), and a pandemic of race hatred that's affected this country for over 400 years. Several vaccines have recently been developed to hopefully get the pandemic caused by the virus under control. I pray for a vaccine for the spirit, that one day people who hate based on race or "any" human difference will receive a shot of love and empathy, and learn that at the end of the day, the only kind of cultural capita(o)l that matters is the kind that honors our unique cultures and unites us in our fragile and temporary humanness.

Notes

1 Cole, N.L. (2019, September 23). *What is cultural capital? Do I have It?* ThoughtCo. https://www.thoughtco.com/what-is-cultural-capital-do-i-have-it-3026374.
2 Baldwin, J. (1998.) *Collected essays* (T. Morrison, Ed. p. 432). Library of America.
3 Alexander, M. (2010). *The new Jim Crow: Mass incarceration in the age of color blindness* (p. 6). The New Press.
4 Alexander, M. (2010). *The new Jim Crow: Mass incarceration in the age of color blindness* (p. 7). The New Press.
5 Geary, D. (2015, September 14). The Moynihan Report: An annotated edition. *The Atlantic.* https://www.theatlantic.com/politics/archive/2015/09/the-moynihan-report-an-annotated-edition/404632/
6 Weems, M. (2008). *Writings of healings and resistance* (pp. 13–15). Peter Lang Publishing.
7 Weems, M. (2008). *Writings of healings and resistance* (p. 71). Peter Lang Publishing.

12

119

Mary E. Weems

Characters:

Darrell Johnson, Black, Late 40s

Juanita Johnson, Black, Late 40s

(Setting: Late at night, in the bedroom of the Johnsons' home on the eastside of Cleveland. At open, Zoom screen is dark, and a loud, raspy, COVID cough can be heard. Husband and wife appear on screen, seated side-by-side at the edge of their bed. He is wearing black exercise sweatpants and a top; she's wearing a loose red top, black pants, and a bright red scarf on her head.)

DARRELL: Baby, that cough sounds like it's getting worse…I'm worried about you.

JUANITA: You've been worried about me damn near since the day we started dating.

DARRELL: That's because you crazy, and I knew I had to keep you on God's mind 24/7.

JUANITA: Uh-Huh. I see you got jokes.

DARRELL: I'm laughing to keep from crying.

JUANITA: Crying about what? What's wrong darlin'?

DARRELL: What's wrong? Nita, you've been coughing hard for the last week, sleeping a lot, hardly eating and now every time I check your forehead, it's hot, plus –

JUANITA: D, don't even go there. I know what you're about to say and I'm not hearing it. I'm feeling better today than I did yesterday and I felt better yesterday than the day before. This cough is not much worse than when my bronchitis kicks in. All this news about COVID just has you scared.

DARRELL: Naw, Nita I'm not scared, I'm terrified. Have you seen the latest reports about how fast it's spreading?

DOI: 10.4324/9781003203520-12

JUANITA: No, because I don't watch that shit like you do. I have my own sources and Ms. Reynolds says white folks are just trying to trick us.

DARRELL: Baby, why are you listening to that old conjure woman about this?

JUANITA: You are getting on my nerves now, D.

DARRELL: Only because you don't want to admit you need to go to the hospital.

JUANITA: So what? Point is, I'm feeling better.

DARRELL: Then why can't I tell?

(Juanita continues like she hasn't heard him.)

JUANITA: I've always been a little hot blooded.

DARRELL: Baby, what the hell are you talking about?

JUANITA: I mean my temperature's always ran a little high…Ms. Reynolds says it's because I'm Black.

DARRELL: That's some bullshit. 98.6 is normal, period.

JUANITA: I understand what you're saying. I used to believe that was true too, but then I met Ms. Reynolds and started studying with her.

DARRELL: Will you please stop talking to me about Ms. Reynolds?

(Juanita begins coughing again uncontrollably.)

DARRELL: Okay, that's it. I'm dialing 911, you need to go to the hospital.

(He reaches in his pocket for his cell phone to dial as Juanita continues talking.)

JUANITA: You can call all you want to, D, but I'm not going anywhere. I keep telling you I'm feeling better every day. I have some of Ms. Reynolds special tonic, I can call her whenever I get ready and –

DARRELL: Hello, hello? Yes, this is Darrell Johnson and my wife is very sick and needs to go to the hospital. My address is 2507 E. 86th Street, Cleveland, Ohio, 44105. Okay, please hurry! Baby if you need to go to the bathroom before they get here, go. I'll get your hat and street shoes.

JUANITA: D, I told you, I'm not –

DARRELL: Nita, you are going. I don't care what you say, you're not getting better and we need to get you checked out. Get ready.

(Screen goes to Black and the sound of ambulance sirens can be heard. A few moments later, Darrell appears on the screen. He's talking with the EMT drivers who can't be seen.)

DARRELL: Hi, please come right in. Thanks for getting here so quickly. Yes, she's in the back, in our bedroom. Right this way. *(Beat)* Yes, she can talk, she's just mad. Please help me get her out of here. *(Beat)* What? You can't take her? Why? This *is* an emergency. What you mean, she's not sick enough? You're not doctors. Your job is to come when people call for help and take them to the goddamn hospital, so please do your damn job and help my wife…Overwhelmed? What? You can't take anyone in unless you think they're sick enough because COVID patients have taken up all the space? Well, what am I supposed to do? My wife has all the symptoms and she's getting worse fast. *(Beat)* Where are you all going? You can't leave. Please,

I'm begging you, please slow down and come back and get my wife, we need help.

(The sound of the front door being slammed can be heard.)

DARRELL: Nita, you believe these bastards refused to take you?

JUANITA: Baby, please try to calm down. Don't get mad at them, they're just doing their job. If the hospital says don't bring people unless they're damn near dead, what are they supposed to do?

DARRELL: Fuck them. All I care about right now is getting you to the hospital. Let's get out of here.

(Screen goes to black and the sound of the front door closing can be heard.)

(Hours later. Darrell is seated on the edge of the bed. The scarf Juanita was wearing is around his neck. He turns to talk to his wife, who's in bed and asleep and can't be seen. He takes her scarf from around his neck and begins tying it in knots as he talks)

DARRELL: She was so glad to get back home…haven't seen her smile like that in over two weeks. She hates hospitals anyway…Lord, please help me. What am I going to do? She's getting sicker, hospitals won't take her. Please help me Father. Please don't take my baby…don't know what I'd do in this world without her.

(He bows his head to pray silently for a few moments, takes out his phone and calls his dad.)

DARRELL: Hello, dad? I know. Sorry to call you so late, but I dialed 911 to get help for Nita and they wouldn't take her. I need your advice.

The End

13

BLACK TRAUMA

Bryant Keith Alexander

My younger sister, who works in the medical care field in a hospital in Louisiana, texted me to ask:

> *December 13, 2020*
> SHE: "They are giving the vaccine here starting Monday. Are you taking it? U taking that vaccine?"
> ME: "Yes, when it becomes available to me. You?"
> SHE: "I just don't know."

Her response reveals the specter of Black suspicion, an element of Black trauma from the histories of the Black experience in America. Not just slavery – if one can ever use such a construction as "just slavery" and not recognize the ways in which slavery has shaped every aspect of the Black experience in these United States of America – but also the physiological, psychological, sociological, cultural, economic, and diasporic split of family and bloodlines. There is also a disturbing history of African Americans being used for medical experimentation that undergirds that suspicion.[1] *The Black body as Guinea pig before white medical application. The Black body as sexual spectacle.*[2] *The Black body as souvenir, with digits of fingers, toes, and penises strewn on neckless as keepsakes after lynching, or being tarred and feathered.*[3] *The Black body as fascination in life and death, like Sister Sara Baartman.*[4] Or the immortal human cells grown in culture, which are still alive today, taken from Henrietta Lacks without her knowledge in 1951 as she was dying from cervical cancer.[5] These stolen cells became one of the most important tools in medical history, allowing important strides toward developing the polio vaccine; researching cancer, viruses, and the atom bomb's effects; and advances in vitro fertilization, cloning, and gene mapping. They have been bought and sold by the

DOI: 10.4324/9781003203520-13

billions, leaving a legacy that far exceeds the care that she received in the hemisphere of her life.

And speaking of celestial forms, the *blackbody* was thought to be "an ideal body that allows all incident radiation to pass into it (zero reflectance) and that absorbs internally all the incident radiation (zero transmittance)."[6] Viewed problematically throughout American history as an anti-template of white anatomy, the Black body has been used to "explain" widely believed abnormalities and deficiencies of Black intellect and proportions, while also being treated as "close enough" in its humanness to serve as foil for experimentation: a less valued specimen of sacrifice for white sustainability. Ultimately, *killing the Black body* has been a sport of white witness – a performance of race and representation in addition to medicalization.[7]

Black suspicion was most heightened following the Tuskegee Study. "The goal was to 'observe the natural history of untreated syphilis' in black populations, but the subjects were completely unaware and were instead told they were receiving treatment for bad blood, when in fact, they received no treatment at all."[8] "Bad blood" like the aphorisms that Black people have "sugar in the blood" or "temperatures that run high." Such folk characterizations might be grounded in a truth of diabetes or high blood pressure, but they stand outside the formality of medical intervention from fear of annihilation through medical genocide.

The distrust for the medical establishment that my sister expressed, and which makes so many Black folks in America hesitant to take the new coronavirus vaccine, is both hereditary and learned.[9] The fact is that "historically, one of the large connections is that, if you're talking about the appropriation of African-American bodies when enslavement was part of the law of the land, that represented an extension of slavery into eternity."[10]

★★★

My younger sister, who works in the medical care field in a hospital in Louisiana, texted me to say:

> January 4, 2021
> HER: "Morning love, I just took the first dose of the vaccine. I am looking for horns to come out.
> ME: Thank God! That you took the first dose, not the horns,

We joke to warn off the ghosts and goblins of our historical past.

Notes

1 Rothm, L. (April 21, 2017). The Disturbing History of African-Americans and Medical Research Goes Beyond Henrietta Lacks. *Times*. https://time.com/4746297/henrietta-lacks-movie-history-research-oprah/. Washington, H. H. (2018). *Medical*

apartheid: The dark history of medical experimentation of black American from Colonial Times to the present. Anchor.

2 Adekunle, T. (n.d.). *Why is the black female body a spectacle?* https://www.johnbyrneaward.org.uk/entries/why-is-the-black-female-body-a-spectacle/, accessed January 7, 2021.

3 Young, H. (2020). The black body as Souvenir, museum, and living remain. In *Embodying Black Experience: Stillness, Critical Memory, and the Black Body* (167–208). University of Michigan.

4 Crais, C. C., & Scully, S. (2009). *Sara Baartmand and the Hottentot venus: A ghost story and a biography.* Princeton University Press; Davie, Lucille (May 14, 2012). Sarah Baartman, at rest at last. *SouthAfrica.info.* Archived from the original on 14 August 2010. Retrieved August 6, 2012; https://www.lucilledavie.co.za/post/2017/04/25/sarah-baartman-at-rest-at-last; Qureshi, S. (2004).Displaying Sara Baartman, the "Venus Hottentot". *History of Science, 42*(136), 233–257. doi:10.1177/007327530404200204. S2CID 53611448. Crais, C. & Scully, P. (June 2009). Hendrik Cesars and the Tragedies of Race in South Africa. Wonders and Marvels; Lederman, Muriel, & Bartsch, I. (2001). *The gender and science reader* (p. 351). Routledge; Strother, Z.S. (1999). Display of the Body Hottentot. In B. Lindfors (Ed.), *Africans on stage: Studies in ethnological show business* (pp. 1–5). Bloomington, Indiana: Indiana University Press; Scully, P. & Crais, C. (2008). Race and Erasure: Sara Baartman and Hendrik Cesars in Cape Town and London. *Journal of British Studies, 47*(2), 301–323. doi:10.1086/526552.

5 Sklott, R. (2011). *The immortal life of Henrietta Lacks*, Crown, cited in the Lily Rothm, *Times* article.

6 Blackbody. https://www.sciencedirect.com/topics/engineering/blackbody; *From: Encyclopedia of Physical Science and Technology* (Third Edition), 2003.

7 Roberts, D. (1998). *Killing the black body: Race, reproduction, and the meaning of liberty.* Vintage Press.

8 Blackbody. https://www.sciencedirect.com/topics/engineering/blackbody; *From: Encyclopedia of Physical Science and Technology* (Third Edition), 2003.

9 Corbi-Smith, G., Thomas S.B., Williams, M. V., and Moody-Ayers, S. (1999). "Attitudes and beliefs of African Americans toward participation in medical research," *Journal of General Internal Medicine, 14*(9), 537–546. https://www.ncbi.nlm.nih.gov/pmc/articles/PMC1496744/; Scharff, D. P., Mathewas, K. J., Jackson, P., Hosssuemmer, J., Martin, E., & Edwards, D. (2020). More than Tuskegee: Understanding mistrust about research participation. *Journal of Health Care for Poor and Underserved, 21*(3), 879–897.

10 Sklott, R. (2011). *The immortal life of Henrietta Lacks*, Crown, cited in the Lily Rothm, *Times* article.

SECTION III
Introduction to Reimagining

Bryant Keith Alexander and Mary E. Weems

We love the notion of black futurity *black futurity* or a or a Black utopia *Black utopia*.

"Within the history of African-American struggle against racist oppression that often verges on dystopia, a hidden tradition has [has always] depicted a transfigured world. Daring to speculate on a future beyond white supremacy, black utopian artists and thinkers offer powerful visions of ways of being that are built on radical concepts of justice and freedom. They (we) imagine a new black citizen who would inhabit a world that soars above all existing notions of the possible."[1]

While Black folks are not a monolith, this notion of a Black utopia does represent a collective consciousness in the spirit of a hope that empowers the struggle for possibility.

The project of futurity and utopia both reimagine the past and projects possible futures. It asks: What in the storied histories of your life, or your people, would you like to reimagine; to rethink, to know, to see, to have experienced differently; to recreate? What historical script would you like to flip? How would you practice the volition of your voice in acting on your reimagination of your own possibility?

These are basic, but not simple, questions that we must all ask of ourselves at some point. They represent the first step in reckoning with the past so we can plan for better ways of being.

What dramas of everyday living would you like to re-write/re-right, re-scripting the roles to speak back to that moment? Would you change the characters and play a different role? Or would you keep your role and find new ways of transforming the scene? What parts of yourself would you keep, and what parts would you refresh? What would you say that you wanted to say, but didn't; what would you do that you wanted to do, but couldn't? What would have been those constraints, and how would you free yourself?

DOI: 10.4324/9781003203520-103

These are questions of reimagining that become rehearsals for living a new.

For what cause would you stand in a duel – stand for the count and chance the outcomes for your reimagined future? What would be your investment in asking for "a little something extra" for your labor, for your loyalty, or for your love?

Write yourself into these questions!

In the song that others have written to narrate your life, what lyrics would you change?

How would you pray differently if the sins of the past were corrected? How would you spell *emancipation* differently once you had it? How would you re-imagine the *decorums of human sociality*, meaning the rules of human engagement in the **race** for superiority? How would you realign the reductive gender rules of masculine/feminine, man/woman, and top/bottom that signify value and worth, completely negating all other free-flowing options and dispositions that exist both between and beyond?

To ask the question is to reimagine the possibilities of living – then to act on that dream.

14

TALKIN' ON A 20 DOLLA BILL

Mary E. Weems

Characters:

HARRIET TUBMAN: Short, dark skinned, elderly Black woman dressed as she appears historically. She wears a long white apron with large pockets. Her revolver is in the right pocket.

ANDREW JACKSON: Tall, white, Elder man dressed as he appears historically in military dress. He has an Indian Treaty in one breast pocket and a dueling pistol in the other.

SETTING: Stage is set with a large American flag hanging on the black wall. Two stools are arranged with one downstage center and the other to the left, approximately two feet behind the first stool, to give the impression that Jackson is "behind" Tubman on the back of the bill.

(*Tubman enters first and takes a seat on the stool. She sits dead still with her hands in her lap. Jackson waits until she's in position, then enters and takes a seat on the other stool. They are unaware of each other and cannot hear or see each other at this point.*)

ANDREW JACKSON: Nigra, bring me my boots!

HARRIET TUBMAN: When I was a chile massa used to beat me for everything and nothin'. Seem like nothin' I did was okay. Didn't allow us to wear clothes till we got old enough to start breedin,' so I was always naked as day I was born, my skin striped like a flag, bruised, cut up.

JACKSON: Where did that mud come from, didn't I tell you to clean them last night?

(*He makes the gesture of whipping a slave.*)

JACKSON: Get your ass out of here and clean 'em right now. Send your mama in here on your way out. I need a bath drawn. Wash this battle dirt off. Hurry up.

DOI: 10.4324/9781003203520-14

TUBMAN: Been old a long time now. Don't remember my birthdate. I was new to the world and nobody around took time to record it. My mother probably had to get right back to work. Seen plenty pitney born like that, dropped in the field like a small pile – a brown cotton, wiped off and took to one – a the old slaves too old to work, the mother rushed back to the field without even time to breastfeed till after work was done.

JACKSON: In battle, boots are very important. They keep your feet dry on cold, wet, rainy, or snow days; they keep them warm at night after a long days' killin'. Boots come in handy when you got a savage on his knees, swift kick to the face can be very persuasive when you want information on where the rest of his tribe are hidin' out.

TUBMAN: Massa. Can I talk to you about somethin'? (*Listens for a moment*) Thank you suh. Well, I know what I want, just not sho quite how to say it, but it's about a little somethin' extra. (*Listens for a moment*) Extra what? Yes suh, that's a good question. Ahm talkin' bout a little somethin' extra for me. (*Listens for a moment*) Extra for what? Yes, suh, another good question. What I mean suh is, remember when you tol' me a while back that if I evah got the money, earned fair and square after I've done everything thing you want me to do, I could buy me? (*Listens for a moment*) That's right suh, my freedom. (*Listens for a moment*) Naw suh, I don't know what I do with it, but one thing I know, it must be somethin' mighty special cause everybody white I know got it and everybody Black I know don't.

JACKSON: Treaty? Man what are you talking about? Have you taken leave of your senses? (*Listens for a few moments*) I don't care what I said to those savages, what did I tell you and all my other men before I met with them? What have you heard me say time and time again 'in private?' (*Listens for a few moments*) That's right. This is white man's land, God sent us here to save it, to teach the ones we can how to survive, kill the ones we can't, tellin' them anything we think they wanta here to get their land. (*Listens for a few moments*) Can you hear, Lieutenant? I said anything. Now get outta here and let's get ready for my surprise at dawn. Dismissed.

TUBMAN: Massa that let me buy my freedom at $50 dollas a year wasn't the first one. Massa Bodras nevah woulda done that. Freed my mother, but nevah told me. Was plannin' to sell me but died befo' he could make it happen. I thanked God at the time. Had heen prayin' for dat man to die every night and every mornin' and every time I thought about it since I learned to pray.

JACKSON: Not takin' prisoners today corporal. Kill 'em. Kill 'em all. (*Listens for a moment*) No, burn it all. Children? Man, what will we do with them afterwards? This is war! Kill 'em. Kill 'em all and don't come back till all you can smell is Indians. Dead ones.

(*Suddenly a voiceover of a Black woman singing the Star-Spangled Banner begins playing. Both Tubman and Jackson stop, look up, and begin singing with the song.*)

BOTH: "Oh Say does that Star Spangled banner yet wave, o'er the Land of the Free and the home of the Brave."

TUBMAN: Massa Bodras started rentin' me out to other places dat didn't have dey own slaves from time I was bout five years old. I'm all Africa, mama and daddy both came from West Africa, a tribe called Ashanti. Dey was warriors and from stories I heard from time I was old enough to listen, dey didn't take no mess. Believed in fightin'.

(Jackson takes the rolled-up Treaty out of his breast pocket and holds it in his fist as he talks.)

JACKSON: Not sure what's wrong with some of these white folks. All this talk about the abolition of slavery, about slavery being wrong, being against God. God? Don't they know this is all God's plan for his people? Haven't they read their Bible where it talks about the white man's responsibility to take care of the lowly? Well what's lower than a nigra? Closest thing to an ape I've ever seen. Even redskins a step or two above 'em. One of the first things I learned. Ben Franklin was right, God meant this country for whites. (*Unrolls treaty between his legs*) Not sure why in the world Indians trusted a piece of paper they let us write. When I was in charge, I drew up a lot of these documents knowing from the moment they were signed, they weren't worth any more than my word. (*Rolls it back up and tosses it over his shoulder*)

TUBMAN: One-a the first things I learnt was the value of a dolla. Everywhere I was, it was almost the only thing that mattered when it came to us. How much it cost to buy us, how much it cost to feed us, how much work could we do for the massa, how much money could he make off us. So, I never knowed nothin' but work. Didn't like housework, always somebody around watchin', includin' some-a my own who'd run and tell da massa or da misses if dey saw anything dat didn't look right. Like somebody tryin' to get away. Liked to be outside, hard work plowin', layin' brick, plantin' and harvestin' crops. Be so tired by the time it was ovah all I could do was eat, pray, and go to sleep.

JACKSON: Funny how killin' Indians and slavery went together like two matching gloves on a pair of hands. Had to get rid of the Indians to get their land, had to get their land so we could have more slaves. This was a hard-scrabble country. Everything here new, and unknown. Too much work for white men alone, too much work for the whole white race. Slaves were only more important than horses cause they cost a lot more, could understand more, and you could whip 'em, torture 'em, and make 'em work when a horse would refuse to move when it was too tired to go on. Plus, once you paid for 'em and deducted for upkeep. Nigras brought a lot more profit, especially nigra women.

TUBMAN: Nevah foget look on my old massa's face, day I showed up wit da money to buy my freedom. You'd a thought he was about to die. Face got red as a just-picked tomato, then pale as a peeled potato all in the same few seconds. I just stood there, holdin' out my hand every dolla down to the coin, what we'd agreed on. He asked me to wait for 'em and left the room for what seemed like fo'eva, I'm guessin' to count it. I was so excited I couldn't even sit down. Thought about all dem years of work, workin' and savin' and sendin' word to my parents, let 'em know I was comin' soon as I could to get 'em to make a place we could all live together so I could take care of 'em.

JACKSON: Loved killin'. Killed more than my share. Indians, prisoners of war, never did understand why we should feed and clothe people we were fighting, so whenever I was in charge, if even one of 'em even looked at me wrong, I had 'em shot. One time, toward the end of the Civil War, word was gettin' around that the war was over. I hadn't got any official message though so it wasn't. One morning six of my men decided they were done with war, wanted to go home and tried to leave before their time was up. Had 'em all shot. Didn't even ask their names before I did it.

TUBMAN: I hated slavery. Thanks to laws and a lot of scared colored and white folks, I nevah learned to read. Thanks to God, I didn't have to, always knew what was right. Everybody the same in his eyes, everybody supposed to be free to live and be happy includin' colored folks and women. Did all I could long as I could to fight. Once I got free, I went back South more 'n 19 times. Freed all the family I could find, freed all the slaves I never met I could find. Made it my business to know what was what on every plantation in the south, learned the Underground Railroad and travelled it, always in the dead of night to get folks out, nevah hesitatin' to lie to white folks, dress up in disguises, and threaten to shoot anybody I freed who even talked about quittin'. Kept my revolver oiled, loaded and knew how to use it. Was a suffragist too, but didn't let white women get away wit tryin' to get they freedom wit-out us. Some-a dem had da nerve to be racist too, but I told 'em all we been through worse than any of you and got just as much right to our freedom as you do to yours. So either we work together, or I work wit da ones who believe like I do – we all tryin' to head to the same place, startin' with da right to vote.

JACKSON: Once we finally moved all the Indians we didn't kill to land we didn't want, we made rules to make it hard for 'em to survive. Some folks called one long trip the Trail of Tears, but only tears I know about were ones them savages shed. It was all I could do not to throw a party. Even though we'd killed damn near 90% of all of 'em, we made sure the rest of 'em would have a real hard time. Took away most of their land, right to vote, and once gold was discovered on what they had left, we passed a law making it illegal for 'em to dig for it. When I was president, I did my best to make certain slavery would last. When I found out them damn abolitionist were sending anti-slavery writings by mail, I worked with the postmaster to stop it.

(*Tubman has fallen asleep. She wakes slowly.*)

TUBMAN: When I was child, one-a the overseers got mad at young Joe, not sure why, I was busy tryin' to finish cleanin' the yard. All of a sudden, I felt a horseshoe smash me in the forehead, don't remember nothin' after that, folk tol' me later I passed out, and stayed out for a few days. After that, I had this gash in my head and I fall asleep any time without feelin' tired.

JACKSON: States rights are always more important than what the government wants. Never could understand the purpose of paper money. Makes no sense whatsoever to take something that's only worth a few cents 'paper,' put a number on it and say that's what it's worth for doing all kinds of business. That's like telling someone you're rich because you just learned how to print paper money, and have made up thousands of dollars. What's it really worth? What's holding it up? I mean if I have a gold coin, I can take it anywhere and somebody will trade me for it based on how much its worth. Paper money is bad news, a disaster waiting to happen. Worthless.

TUBMAN: I nevah knew what it was to think like one person. Used to hear white folks talk about bein' a individual, and workin' against each other to be what they called successful, and how bein' a American meant lookin out fo yoself. I don't think I could sleep if I felt like that. Always thinkin' bout how to work to help somebody else. When I was a spy for the Union I'd creep around the South, listenin' to everything I could from the Confederates then take it right back to the Union spillin' my guts, tryin' to make it easier for all colored folks to get dey freedom. One time I was in charge. I knew the lay of de land, all the plantation overseers, everything. Led a group of colored soldiers into battle, whooped de other sides behind and freed 700 slaves at one time. Didn't count 'em but dat's what I heard later. Hmph, when the war was over Gover'ment refused to even give me my pay for servin', but dat didn't stop me, it ended slavery and that made it all worth it, besides I knew long as I could work, I'd be alright cause that's why God put me here, work and helping colored people. Always believed in business. Watched how white folks used us to build de fortune and learned quick. After de war I got paid for teachin' former slaves how to work and get paid, ran a brick yard, grew and sold vegetables, ran a hog farm. Always knew that money equal power. After I was bought and sold twice, used money bought myself outta slavery. Bought property, retired, took care-a my mother and father, started a place for old Black folks, then lived there myself when I got tired. Money is the root, Never forgot that matter-a fact –

(*Tubman is interrupted by:*)

VOICEOVER REPORTER: Today, the United States Treasury department made history when it announced that Andrew Jackson, slave-owning, Indian-killing, treaty-breaking bastard, hater of paper money, seventh president of the United States, would be replaced on the 20-dollar bill by Harriet

Tubman, former slave, freer of slaves, Civil War hero, abolitionist, suffragist, and entrepreneur. Jackson has been moved to the back of the bill.

(*Tubman immediately jumps up, puts her hand in her apron pocket and turns to face Jackson, who is standing and beginning to move toward her. Tubman begins circling backward as Jackson moves toward her until the two are at opposite ends of the stage in dueling stance.*)

JACKSON: Nigger wench, what are you doing looking at me in the eye?

(*Silence*)

JACKSON: What's wrong are you deaf?

(*He begins to reach for his breast pocket. Tubman pulls her revolver.*)

TUBMAN: Make another move and it'll be the last thing you do.

(*Jackson takes his hand down to his side.*)

JACKSON: Do you have any idea who you're talking to, darkie?

TUBMAN: Yes. Seems to me I just heard a voice from Heaven identify you as a slave-owning, India- killin', treaty-breakin' bastard by the name – a Andrew Jackson.

JACKSON: Heaven be damned. I don't know where that noise came from but I'm certain Heaven had nothin' to do with it, and if you're one of those anti-slavery abolitionists, you're lucky you have a gun on me.

TUBMAN: And if I didn't? You think I'm afraid-a a white man like you? Shoot, I cut my teeth on men like you, startin' wit the first man who bought me like I was a horse. (*She raises her arm and points her gun at his genitals.*) Beat me regular from time I was a chile, raped me, raped damn near every slave woman he owned. You think I'm worried bout you? You just another colored folks hatin' white man, worth less to me than bullets in this gun. What I wanta know about is what the voice meant by puttin' me on a 20 dollar bill and kickin' you off the front and puttin' you on the back. What does dat mean? Sounds like all kinda crazy to me.

JACKSON: Don't know and don't care. It's worthless as –

TUBMAN: You are, breathin' de same air with me.

(*Jackson is silent.*)

TUBMAN: What's dat you got in yo' breast pocket?

(*Jackson begins to reach for it without answering.*)

TUBMAN: One more move and I'll treat you like you did the Indians, kill you where you stand.

JACKSON: I ain't afraid of you, I've been shot before. Get on with it.

TUBMAN: First, slowly reach in that pocket and let me see what you got.

(*Jackson takes his dueling pistol out and holds it at his side.*)

TUBMAN: Duelin' pistol? So I see you like to duel. Okay, I've never had a duel, but I do know how to shoot, let's me and you try this duelin' think out. I'll even let you shoot first. Call it.

JACKSON: I'll fire on the count of ten. One, two, three, four, five, six, seven –

(Tubman shoots Jackson in the heart before he reaches ten. He drops to the ground like a sack of potatoes in front of her. Tubman looks at him for a minute, steps 'on' then over his body, andy turns to face the audience.)

TUBMAN: I lied.

(She walks back over him, then turns to look back at his body.)

TUBMAN: And get off my back.

(She walks upstage and stands in front of the flag at its center.)

Note

1 Zamalin, A. (2019). *Black Utopia: The history of an idea from black nationalism to Afrofuturism.* Columbia University Press.

15
LAGNIAPPE

Bryant Keith Alexander

When I was growing up in southwest Louisiana, there was a tradition of giving called *lagniappe*. Like a baker's dozen, it's *a little something extra given*. In my childhood experience, the local corner store owner in my neighborhood gave it to customers or children: a free piece of candy, a piece of chewing gum, or maybe a cookie or pickle from the jar or jug. Later, when making purchases for my mother or grandmother, it was that couple extra slices of summer luncheon meat or bologna, to keep the kids fed when out of school. In restaurants, it was a cup of crawfish bisque or gumbo with the meal. Or with day laborers, it was a little more pay than the agreed-upon amount. In polite company, it was not something asked for, but something given in exchange for loyalty: a treat for the well-mannered child, extra reward for a job well done, or just a gesture of *southern hospitality*.

Southern hospitality is a social construction created by whites based on their own imagined performance of gentility in relation to their own sense of self, for plantations in the South offered no direct aspects of hospitality for slaves.[1] Black people don't – or shouldn't – talk about *southern hospitality*, because we have been on the receiving end of that stick through the performativity of slavery.

But under certain conditions, when the labor of engagement had far exceeded the expected human spirit, and when the offer of *lagniappe* was not immediately forthcoming, it was requested with a coy politeness, so as to not overstep the propriety of etiquette. *Lagniappe* was asked for as consideration of good spirit, and not demanded as compensation. The ask was a delicate balance within the *decorum of politeness*.

I have imagined different circumstances in the *decorum of human sociality* in which the anticipation and then asking for "a little something' extra" might test the politics of hierarchical boundaries. It exists between what is expected and what is earned, between the recognition of "a job well done" and a space of entrapment in servitude.

DOI: 10.4324/9781003203520-15

I have imagined different circumstances in the *decorum of human sociality*, where the presumptive issue of power and control outweigh the perceived need to offer sociohuman consideration in acts of care and recognition – with "a little something extra."

I have experienced different circumstances in which the power differentials are not mediated by need – primary to secondary – in a practice of power, in which giving *lagniappe* is seen as a weakness that threatens one's authority.

I have experienced different circumstances in which acceptance or tolerance of my Black, gay, male intellect and spirit does not depend on the "kindness of strangers" – which is a very *southern* construct – and hence can be withheld to keep me in a position of servitude, even with a PhD behind my name.

And I have experienced the modern-day request of *massa* to relieve me of my burden; to set me free for a lifetime of "good behaviors," and even the offer to "buy myself," to "buy my time," to buy back my ability to focus my life spirit to something akin to uplift and freedom.[2]

I have experienced that in the year 2021: in *the year of the* ox, in *the year of activism and resurrection*, in *the year of national atonement*, and maybe *in the year of our Lord* (because I know that he is watching).

I have a clear sense of what I would do with that accumulated set of hopes and dreams and possibilities of my potentialities as a free human being, linked with validating my struggles and working for the liberation and *freedom* of others. Because "I know, it must be somethin' mighty special cause everybody white I know got it and everybody Black I know don't."

I am a man of prayer.

I learned how to pray both under duress from my very Catholic, Black mother, with scars on her back from servitude, and then from an achieved faith and understanding of the possibilities of salvation through faith. Though I also understand that fighten' and faith are not anathema to each other. *Faith requires a little fight*. That is also a part of "God's plan for his people." A persistence of faith needs to be challenged and defended. *That's biblical, Ya'll!*

Dueling with the devil is a lifelong responsibility to which All Black People must attend – no matter the cost or value of the bill!

Notes

1 See: Bryant Keith Alexander (2012). Chapter 2: Southern hospitality indeed!: A performative engagement with art depictions of African American culture in the rural south. In Bryant Keith Alexander (Ed.), *The performative sustainability of race: Reflections on black culture and the politics of identity* (pp. 53–83). Peter Lang Press; McPherson, T. (2003). *Reconstructing Dixie: Race, gender, and nostalgia in the imagined south*. Duke University Press.

2 The reader should of course recognize the dialogue between this piece and Mary E. Weems' "Talkin' on a 20 Dolla Bill" in this volume.

16

I AM A WOMAN OF PRAYER

Mary E. Weems

I learned how to pray from my maternal grandmother, number one fan and teacher about life. Anytime my two sisters and brother spent the night at her house during the 13 years we lived with mama, who'd had all four of us before her 21st birthday and was divorced by the time I was about seven years old, granny had us get on our knees by the side of the fresh-made bed, fold our hands together, and say: "Now I lay me down to sleep, I pray the Lord my soul to keep. If I should die before I wake, I pray the Lord my soul to take," followed by silent prayers for our mother and anyone else each of us wanted God to give special attention to.

Even though my grandmother and all 10 of her siblings were raised in the Baptist Church, she never talked to us about religion, or read to us from the Bible. Also, even though most of her siblings and their children were raised in the church, mama and my uncle Butch were not, and my grandmother never attended church during my lifetime. I'm not sure if I was told this or made the assumption at some point, but since my grandfather, who never talked about religion with us – he was a man of few words and the strongest/best man I've ever known – didn't attend church, and he and my grandmother were close as an endless kiss, I think his lack of interest in organized religion is the reason this foundation was lacking in our branch of the Owens family.

My grandmother did make sure I was baptized, though. One day, granny's sister – my late Auntie Ethel – called after we'd moved into my grandparents' four-bedroom house so mama could work the third shift at her new factory job at Stouffer's. She asked granny if she could take me to church to be baptized. It was an unforgettable, scary experience. The church had an indoor baptismal pool, and without any explanation, I was told to get dressed in this white sheet and summarily dumped in the ice-cold water, while the pastor said words I couldn't

DOI: 10.4324/9781003203520-16

understand because I was terrified. I've never told anyone how I felt – not my auntie on the ride back to granny's house, or my grandmother, or anyone else. I assumed this was good for me, because if it wasn't, auntie Ethel wouldn't have called granny, and she wouldn't have agreed to it.

Like my brother, Bryant, though I am a deeply spiritual person, I believe that there are many paths to a God in whom we both deeply believe. I pray each night while lying in my bed, always beginning with, "Now I lay me down to sleep," always ending with asking God to ease the suffering of the sick and continue to watch over this world.

Unlike the few folks I know who are atheist, I experience God's presence on a daily basis and will never forget how close I felt to God's spirit on March 4, 1983, when my daughter entered this world through the wide-open portal of my body. When we were moved into a warm room filled with soft blue light, and the nurse laid her little body on my chest so I could breast feed her for the first time, I knew God was in that space with us, that I was blessed beyond my wildest dreams to have the privilege of becoming a mother. In addition to the miracle of the things that happen in nature and all of the things which happen that humankind cannot explain – including how the mind-body and spirit work – my ability to write is another constant reminder of God's existence, love, and support. I wouldn't be able to continue to thrive in this world without it.

17

O' FOR MY GRAND/MOTHER

Bryant Keith Alexander

My mother and my grandmother both knew my gender was fluid, maybe long before I had given words to it. They only *knew that my description could not fit their tongue, and I would have a certain way of being in this world* – think Maya Angelou.[1]

That's part of the witchy ways of mothers and grandmothers that people sometimes call intuition, but an intuition that was gestated for nine months, then further *breast fed,* nurtured, and observed as an extension of the self. My mother of her son, and my grandmother through the pregerminated seeds of her son, my father, his mother.

Two women who I never thought really liked each other in the generational mother/mother-in-law dialectic. But each loved me, and each saw me first.

Each *made sure that I was baptized.*
Each made sure that I went to Church every Sunday.
Each made sure that I went to catechism.
Each made sure that I was confirmed – then an altar boy, choir boy, church lecturer.
Each wanting to make sure God was in my life –
not to change me,
not to reimagine me,
but to fulfill the grace of God within me.

To ensure that the trinity of *the mind-body-spirit* was activated in me and my relationship with *the father, the son, and the holy spirit* in a form of respect for each in relation to the other – and myself.

DOI: 10.4324/9781003203520-17

My mother and grandmother each whispered greatness in my ears, each imagining a world that would embrace their boy/man/woman/child. *I too wouldn't be able to continue to thrive in this world without it.*

Note

1 Angelou, M. (1991). For our grandmothers. In *I shall not be moved* (pp. 33–37). Bantam Books.

18

O! SAY CAN YOU SEE?

Mary E. Weems

Fourteen days after the violent insurrection at the State Capitol, on January 20, 2021, the event the attack was designed to stop happened right on schedule. Joseph R. Biden was sworn in as the 46th President of the United States, and in another history making moment I've lived long enough to see, Kamala Harris – our first Black, woman Vice President – was sworn in, requiring a new term for her husband, Doug Emhoff: first "Second Gentleman," and the first Jewish spouse of a Vice President. In the midst of a history making election comparable only to the election of Barack Hussein Obama as our first Black president, in the midst of an inauguration ceremony which featured the powerful voice of Amanda Gorman, a young African-American poet and the youngest inaugural poet in US history, thanks to her selection by Dr. Jill Biden, Lady Gaga lent her unique voice and unforgettable persona to singing her version of "The Star-Spangled Banner," our National Anthem.

There was a time I would have chimed in, singing to the television screen, proud to know the words and claiming my right as a descendant of slaves to sing them, filled – despite our nation's ongoing issues with racism and oppression – with the hope of an even better day for the country I love. Unfortunately, like so many things about the actual history of the United States that I didn't learn until I became a doctoral student, I feel differently about it, since I became aware of the **third stanza** of the song:

> And where is that band who so vauntingly swore,
> That the havoc of war and the battle's confusion
> A home and a Country should leave us no more?
> Their blood has wash'd out their foul footstep's pollution.
> No refuge could save the hireling and slave

DOI: 10.4324/9781003203520-18

And the star-spangled banner in triumph doth wave
O'er the land of the free and the home of the brave.

Written by slave owner and anti-abolitionist Francis Scott Key in 1814, the current national anthem started as a poem titled "The Defence of Fort McHenry." It recounts the Battle of Baltimore, a day-long siege between British and American forces which Key witnessed. He became upset that there were Black men fighting on both sides for the same thing the American forces wanted from the British/Crown of England: freedom.

After doing research via CNN.com and theintercept.com[1] to learn more about the history of the song, including why it was selected as our National Anthem, I was surprised to learn that "The Star-Spangled Banner" wasn't formally adopted by Congress until 1931, during segregation and the Great Depression. Within 48 hours of former Pres. Herbert Hoover signing Maryland Rep. John Linthicum's bill making it official, the controversy started. Supporters of "The Star-Spangled Banner" held a parade in Baltimore carrying American and Confederate flags, while Union army veterans dropped out and denounced the rebels for hijacking the parade. A neo-confederate woman accused the Union veterans of being "Un-American and Divisive," a statement which quickly propelled me through the 4 years of the T-rump presidency.

The CNN.com report[2] cites three white male experts who provide a line-by-line analysis of the song: Mark Clague, Associate Professor of Musicology and American Culture at the University of Michigan and co-founder of "The Star Spangled-Banner Music Foundation"; Marc Leepson, American journalist and historian who wrote a biography of Francis Scott Key; and Alan Taylor, a Pulitzer Prize-winning historian specializing in the American colonial revolution and Early Republic.

Two things struck me about their analysis of the third stanza. First, all three of them were white males providing both an objective interpretation based on historical data, and a subjective take on the song based on their interpretation of the data.

Second, all of the interpretations of specific lines were attributed to a specific white, male expert providing analysis, with the exception of this interpretation, the phrase which begins stanza three, "And where is that band." This line is explained without individual attribution: "Key was a slave owner and anti-abolitionist, here he's referring to slaves and their role in the battle on both the American and British side."

This is important, because this is the only segment of the interpretation which references slaves fighting on **both** sides. The individually attributed interpretations only reference slaves fighting for the British.

The experts then turn to the remaining lines of stanza three.

Clague thinks the "slaves" in the phrase "hireling and slave" refers specifically to the enslaved Colonial Marines who escaped American bondage and were offered their freedom in exchange for fighting on the British side. In the next line, Leepson notes that he thinks the phrase "gloom of the grave" is Key speaking as a slave owner who considers the slaves' "betrayal" an unpatriotic act **(unpatriotic? #WTF?)** and threatens them with the "gloom of the grave" to encapsulate his feelings about it.

Clague later notes, "This whole stanza was cut from the National Anthem **because** of its mocking of the **British**. When we became allies with them in WWII, stanza three drops out of use." (Emphasis mine.)

What sick, thick irony knowing that this song, whose third stanza **only** denigrates Black Americans, was abandoned because the United States was concerned about mocking its World War II British allies – who had been the enemy when the song was written – and **not** because it dishonors the contributions of Black soldiers.

Finally, the first line of stanza four reads, "O thus be it ever when freemen shall stand."

Leepson remarks, "I have a problem with the word 'freemen.' He's [Key] talking about white people." Clague responds, "It was a racist era and we can't change the fact that many of our founding documents have racism at their heart, but for me [a white man] 'freemen' refers to whites and [B]lacks."

This is bullshit without any basis in history or fact. It's simply Clague using his white privilege to feign denial of something he could not possibly believe.

According to Marc Leepson, Francis Scott Key's biographer,[3] Key only spoke publicly about "The Star-Spangled Banner" once (without mentioning what he meant by "slave") and never about the song in his surviving letters. Given that this "song" secured Key's significance in US history, this omission begs the question: Why not?

While I'd like to speculate that it was because Key became ashamed of the song in later years, I doubt it, because even if he didn't want to say so publicly, he could have shared any "change" of heart in his private papers.

The Star-Spangled Banner is one of several, key, unjust vestiges of slavery. Another is the electoral college, which had it been eliminated could have saved us from the likes of Trump, even though many would argue that Hillary Clinton only represented the lesser of two evils.

Take a minute to consider what 4 years of Clinton would have been like as compared to Donald J. Trump...

Unlike the reasonable explanation I learned in high school, the electoral college's purpose was not to ensure smaller states were adequately represented in the final decision to elect our president and vice president. It was actually created to allow Southern states to count their slaves as part of their population – albeit at the less-human 3/5 of one white man rate – to increase the impact of the South's voting power, which without it, would have consistently ceded the one-man-one-vote advantage to the North.

Despite passage of the Voting Rights Act in 1965 to protect Blacks' right to vote, another ongoing sign that Black people are not considered equal to whites and other American citizens on any level is the ongoing effort to prohibit, threaten, and limit our ability to vote by almost any means necessary. This is reflected in a constant effort to adjust state laws and practices, including gerrymandering to shape geographical voting blocks to favor one party over the other; limiting the number of polling places and the number of voting machines in heavily populated Black areas; and – in the Trump/Biden election – even going to so far as to sabotage the ability of the US Post Office to deliver the mail in an election year in which the COVID-19 pandemic forced a drastic increase in the number of people voting by mail.

At the end of the Civil War, while Black people who were still slaves were learning slavery had ended, Blacks of the day would praise Abraham Lincoln, thank him publicly and hold him up as their hero, an exemplar of "freedom" – of a better day for Black folks. I recently learned that the Emancipation Memorial Statue of Lincoln, with a shirtless Black man on one knee at his feet, was paid for by grateful freed Black slaves. Yet, Lincoln's true feelings about us are revealed in his private papers and in speeches like this one:

During the 4th of his famous debates with Senator Stephen Douglas for the US Senate seat in Illinois on September 18, 1858, Lincoln said:

> I am not nor ever have been in favor of bringing about in any way the social and political equality of the white and black races. [...] I am not nor ever have been in favor of making voters or jurors of Negroes, nor qualifying them to hold office, nor intermarry with white people; and I will say in addition to this that there is a **physical** difference between the white and black races which I believe will forever forbid the two races from living together on terms of social and political equality. And inasmuch as they cannot so live, while they do remain together there must be a position of superior and inferior, and I as much as any other man am in favor of having the superior position assigned to the white race.[4] (Emphasis mine)

The fact is that the Civil War was **not** fought over freeing Black people, a myth which continues to be taught and perpetuated in the United States today. It was fought over taxation and, in the main, states' rights to preserve the institution of slavery. In the South, the number one asset for most slave-owning white men was their slaves.

BRYANT: Yes Lawd! Asset in the most reductive sense of the term: "property owned by a person or company, regarded as having value and available to meet debts, commitments, or legacies" of the owner.

Also, since the South had seceded from the Union in 1860, Lincoln's Emancipation Proclamation issued on January 1, 1863, was more of a **threat** – a power move to bring the South back to the bargaining table!

Black people in the United States have been singing *We Shall Overcome* as long as I've been in this world, yet 401 years after the first slave ship landed, we live with constant reminders of how far we are from that ever happening. Even most of the paper money and coinage we use includes the images of either former slave owners or people like Abraham Lincoln who believed we were inferior to white folks.

While nowadays I mute "The Star-Spangled Banner" if it's being sung on television or played elsewhere electronically, or refuse to participate if it's being performed somewhere I'm physically present, watching Lady Gaga, mouth the first line was like listening to an old 78 album that got stuck in one groove:

> O! Say can you See! that there was no young Black male poet featured with Amanda Gorman?
> O! Say can you See! the 74 million people who voted for Trump a second time (shamefully 9% of them Black, more than the 8% who voted for him the first time) are waiting for the second coming of a man too ignorant to know Frederick Douglass is dead, too ignorant to know what happened at Pearl Harbor, too heartless to care about tens of thousands of people dying from COVID-19 on his watch – and who celebrated while the thousands of white folks he called to attack the Capitol did so without being stopped?
> O! Say can you See! that Black people have shed our men, women, and children as slaves, our blood, sweat, tears, for a better day; that we still work, struggle, hope, and pray for a change we keep thinking is coming, while counting our innocent dead shot in the back, chest, head, and heart by racist police mixed in with those who protect and serve?
> O! Say can you See! that we remain on the bottom of the bottom in damn near every significant category of having an opportunity to not just be alive but to thrive? Education, employment, economics, home ownership, health. Can you see that we continue to suffer from de facto redlining, de facto school segregation, de facto oppression in spite of laws we fought to have put in place, thinking maybe the racist heart could be forced to see us as deserving – of being an integral part of this land and free?
> O! Say can you See! the devastating impact of going from Slavery, to Convict Leasing, to the Prison Industrial Complex?
> O! Say can you See! that a country this divided cannot continue to stand? That as James Baldwin once said: what happens to Black folks affects everybody, whether acknowledged or not.
> O! Say can you See! that love is more powerful than hate, that WE are not going anywhere, that until all of us are free, **FREEDOM** is just a word?
> O! Say can you See! that "The Star-Spangled Banner" is a song about war, about conquering, about a flag that can wave forever, but until it waves in a country, in a world at peace with itself – I

BRYANT: O! Say can you See! BLACK LIVES MATTER!
Can't see?

Currently, one of the most popular television ads is a Progressive Insurance commercial advertising its motorcycle coverage. In the original and several subsequent renditions, the star is a dark-skinned part man/part machine, his torso carefully positioned on top of a motorcycle. As someone who's been critically conscious of the subtle ways carefully constructed commercials have **always** been used to reinforce negative stereotypes about Black people and others, each time I see it I'm immediately reminded of Article 1, Section 2, Number 3, of the U.S. Constitution of 1787 which reads: "Representatives and direct Taxes shall be apportioned among the several States which may be included within this Union, according to their respective Numbers, which shall be determined by adding to the whole Number of free Persons, including those bound to Service for a Term of Years, and excluding Indians not taxed, **three fifths of all other Persons**." [emphasis added]

I often wonder why there hasn't been an outcry to have this commercial removed, but I suspect it's because too many of us are unaware of the 3/5 human idea the Black man's image references.

BRYANT: The half Black man, half motorcycle is called a "motaur." There is a version of this commercial in which the motaur is perched on a bluff looking down on a herd of "motaurs" of differing ages and ethnicities, running. The motaur looking longingly through binoculars at what is supposed to read as their natural wonder. His sidekick, a white man sitting on a motorcycle next to him, says, "Amazing to see them running in the wild like…" But before he can finish, the motaur raises his hand to hush him, then raises his front wheel in what appears to be a longing salute.

I end with a quote from the writings of one of my late sheroes, the Black, lesbian, feminist warrior poet, Audre Lorde:

> Without a rigorous and consistent evaluation of what kind of a future we wish to create, and a scrupulous examination of the expressions of power we choose to incorporate into all our relationships including our most private ones, we are not progressing, but merely recasting our own characters in the same old weary drama.[5]

Notes

1 Schwarz, J. (2016, August 28). Colin Kaepernick is righter than you know: The national anthem is a celebration of slavery. *The Intercept*. https://theintercept.com/2016/08/28/colin-kaepernick-is-righter-than-you-know-the-national-anthem-is-a-celebration-of-slavery/.

2 Campisi, J., & Willingham, A.J. (n.d.). Behind the lyrics of the Star-Spangled banner. *CNN*. https://edition.cnn.com/interactive/2018/07/us/national-anthem-annotated/.

3 Leepson, M. (2014). *What so proudly we hailed: Francis Scott Key, a life*. St. Martin's Press. See also Francis Scott Key, intercept article.

4 Mr. Lincoln and Negro Equality. (1860, December 28). *The New York Times*. https://www.nytimes.com/1860/12/28/archives/mr-lincoln-and-negro-equality.html.

5 Lorde, A. (1980, April 12). Letter to the editor. *Gay Community News 7:30.*

SECTION IV
Introduction to Reparations

Bryant Keith Alexander and Mary E. Weems

Reparations is a hot-button issue that should be within the realm of all progressive social conscious activities. They occur when any entity, be it private citizen, body politic, country, or sovereign nation, recognizes that a wrong has been perpetrated against friend or foe (or nature), and attempts to "pay back" the aggrieved as a restitution of harm. In the case of slavery, the nonprofit Human Rights Watch approaches reparations with the following logic:

> We begin with the premise that slavery, the slave trade, the most severe forms of racism associated with colonialism, and subsequent official racist practices such as apartheid in South Africa or the Jim Crow laws in the United States are extraordinarily serious human rights violations. If committed today, these would be crimes against humanity. Under traditional and straightforward human rights law and policy, each living victim of these practices is entitled individually to seek and receive reparations from those who committed or permitted these wrongs. By "reparations" we mean not only compensation, but also acknowledgment of past abuses, an end to ongoing abuses, and, as much as possible, restoration of the state of affairs that would have prevailed had there been no abuses.[1]

Within this construction, reparations are linked with crimes against humanity. The compensation for such crimes is both particular and plural, situational and longitudinal, living and historical, embodied and generational, as a right to seek and receive recognition, restitution, or return.

What do you seek reparations for in your personal or cultural history? What price must be paid for what was lost relative to life and liberty, dignity and spirit,

DOI: 10.4324/9781003203520-104

in the middle passages of your willing or unwilling travels? What do you want restored *to the state of affairs that would have prevailed had there been no abuses?*

The modern struggle for reparations is routed in these basic questions of human dignity. And while financial compensations might address current-moment needs – or may invest in new future possibilities for the harmed and aggrieved – what has been lost will not be found. It (they) has long settled at the bottom of oceans, their blood soaking into earth that has regenerated the detritus of human flesh, melding life with nature not to be again recognized, not to be resuscitated or returned.

They only exist as spirits of our remembrance whispering to our souls.

And while we conjure their spirits in writing, we cannot undo their suffering or their loss, nor our loss of them (**whomever "them" is to you, fill in the blank for yourself:________________________**), nor can we recover those lost parts of ourselves that they would have helped us to better understand in our current practiced humanity. How do we add those considerations to the metrics of determining reparations, along with the cost of their labor that has made possible the wealth of others?

19

THE PAYBACK

Bryant Keith Alexander

February 23, 2021

I was taking a walk with my dog, one of the few pleasures of excursion during the COVID-19 pandemic, and I saw a familiar sight: one of several delivery trucks dropping off the vague necessities of living or the follies of impulse-buying online to one of our sequestered neighbors.

As my dog Picklz and I moved closer to the truck, momentarily vacated while the delivery was being made, I heard a familiar song playing on blast coming from it. I immediately recognized the song as James Brown singing, "The Payback." I giggled as I began to sing along. Then I saw the driver, a much younger Black man who was bobbing his head, getting his groove on, as he returned to his truck. We both became caught in a shared moment of nostalgia – or at least I did, *a man of a certain age* who could actually remember back to when the album with the same name dropped in 1973. ***Mary Weems was tickled when I wrote the "Black Notes" piece and used the phrase "people of a certain age." She knows.***

I smiled at the young Black man; we smiled at each other with a knowing recognition of each other's appreciation of the same tune. And I said to him,

> "What do yoooou know about 'The Payback'"?

We both laughed in that way that older Black men always josh younger Black boys as ritual play. And if it is delivered just right, they know you are teasing and trying to connect across generations. And he simply said,

> "This is just good shit, man. And I am waiting for mine."

DOI: 10.4324/9781003203520-19

And I simply said,

> *"O Yeah, Yeah you're right!"*

We waived and moved in opposite directions, each still smiling, still bobbing our heads and still singing.

I smiled for the rest of our walk as I thought about what the young Black man said: "This is just good shit man, and I am waiting for mine." The first part just tickled me in that way that younger people inherit music, like discovering old classic television shows on premium channels, or those who connected to the music from their grandparents. The appreciation is great, but sometimes I just believe that *good shit is good shit* or that *blood and bodies remember* the rhythms and stylistics of our Black history, across generations in a collaboration of spirits. He was cute in his appreciation. My people would say, "He had an old soul."

The second part of his utterance was more curious to me. You see, that classic funk tune "The Payback" tells a loosely constructed narrative where the male singer expresses the revenge he plans to take against a man who betrayed him, with his wife being implicated in the betrayal. The plot is to get "payback." The threat is interwoven in a cyclic groove and a sort of freestyle jamming rant:

> *Hey, gotta, gotta payback! (the big payback)*
> *Revenge!*
> *I'm mad (the big payback)*
> *Got to get back!*
> *Need some get back!*
> *Pay Back! (the big payback)*
> *That's it!*
> *Payback!*
> *Revenge!*
> *I'm mad!*
>
> *You get down with my girlfriend, that ain't right!*
> *Hollerin', cussin', you want to fight*
> *Payback is a thing you gotta see, hey*
> *Brother do any damn thing to me*

The song is rife with James Brown's signature screams, shouts, and grunts, with the sounds of the *wah wah* guitar/pedal that bends and manipulates frequencies, sometimes mimicking the human voice, like a cry or a squeal in a weird call n' response with the singer. In some ways, this is a "somebody done somebody wrong" song. Is that what the young Black man was referencing? Somebody did him wrong, and he was waiting for payback? Then I started thinking more about *payback*; maybe payback as the return of a debt, or maybe payback as reparations. A different kind of "somebody done somebody wrong" song; a different kind of repayment of debt. Though ***Mary Weems also asks: "Maybe James Brown was using allegory to sing about payback/reparations."*** *What a lovely imagining.*

The young Black delivery driver is a Black male in America listening to "The Payback." He said, "and I am waiting for mine." Maybe he was talking about reparations from slavery and its inherent historical effects on all African-American people, leading to the everyday inequities that still require us to profess that, "Black Lives Matter." Effects that lead to the everyday atrocities of violence on Black peoples on the streets and in the safety of our own homes; effects that cause the everyday implicit/explicit biases of our social in/mobilities: getting a job, getting an education, driving, and walking while Black in America (home of the free and the brave?). Just today, today! ***Mary Weems sent me and email that said: "You hear about the young man who was arrested for walking while Black?"*** I turned to the news and the headline read: "Police drop charges after Black teenager arrested while walking home amid a winter storm."[2] A safety check turned problematic. fueled by a *history of* and *resistance to* police violence against Black people in America.

Maybe the young Black male delivery driver was talking about reparations from slavery and histories of degradation of Blacks in this country – even of those of us with BAs, MAs, PhDs, EdDs, and JDs behind our names – who still know that the materiality of our bodies transcend the content of our characters and our accomplishments, contributions, and being in the world.

Mary Weems stated: "We don't have our degrees tattooed on our foreheads." But in dialogue with Mary: would that *even* make a difference? She references the 2009 case of preeminent African-American scholar and Harvard University Prof. Henry Louis Gates, Jr., being arrested when attempting to enter his own home in Cambridge, Massachusetts. Neighbors had reported suspicious activity.

Martin Luther King, Jr.'s, 1963 dream is not realized in the year 2021.[3] And we are more than *three-fifths of a person* – or was that *three-fifths of a citizen* – back then and beyond, and in the present and the future.[4] Each variation is problematic under the Lord and under true democratic ideals, both then and now. We are Black first in America – and we proceed with that caution in every aspect of our personal and professional lives.

Maybe the young Black male delivery agent was talking about reparations in that sense, as *the payback*. What is he waiting for in reparations? What is his list of demands?

R **R**espect, **r**ecognition, **r**econciliation, **r**estitution, **r**eclamation, **r**epatriation
E **E**conomic justice, **e**go identification
P **P**ayments, **p**ower, **p**atronage
A Apology!

R Restoration of dignity, **r**ecognition of national victimage, **r**esolution against white supremacy
A Apology!
T Tax Cuts, **T**rust Funds, **T**reatises, **T**ruce
I Investments **in** Black people, **in** Black businesses, **in** HBCUs, **in** Black Students, **in** Black Futures, **in** the Black Lives That Matter!
O Overt action to **o**vercome **o**ppression in the United States of America for all BIPOC
N Negate the words **nigger/negroid/negro** from the social and political lexicon as references of monolithic negativity, though I do like the term *négritude* as an affirmation of Black consciousness.

Mary Weems writes: Like hurtful words other groups have embraced and found a way of making their own, I "embrace" the word nigger and use it in my speech and writings whenever I want to. Examples: Nigger please! You my nigger. Nigger don't you know you my best friend?

S Systemic racism (eradicated)

I hear him.

I hear him like I heard *the stereophonic Black notes* that he was delivering from his work vehicle – the Black notes *that makes white folks turn their heads* but just made me say, *"Oh Yeah, Yeah you're right!"*

***

I walk through the predominately white neighborhood that I live in. I walk a common path with a guarded ease. There are good white folks with **Black Lives Matter** posters in their yards to whom I waive as we pass, but we never stop. Cute dogs, like good fences, make good neighbors. But I am reminded of two incidents not too long ago, in the same neighborhood, that made me change my path. Each of which make me think about "the payback" in different ways.

"Walking the Dog/Being the Dog"[5]

Throughout my life, my father told me stories about living in the Jim Crow South. Many of these stories hinged on a strained performance of servitude under the lingering privileges of whiteness and the dangers of blackness. My father told "back of the bus" stories and "back door" stories. He told Ku Klux Klan stories and lynching stories. He told, "Don't look at White women stories" and "Don't look the White man in the eye" stories. And, like my father, my mother told "daughter of a sharecropper" stories. She told "being a Black female domestic" stories." And she told "having to care for white babies when her own babies had to go without" stories. The stories they told were not told as entertainment or as fanciful tales of days gone by. These were pained stories that my Black parents told me as lessons, not of their hardship or sacrifice, but of their strategies for survival.

I live in a neighborhood adjacent to the private university campus where I work. Some might describe the neighborhood as upscale.

There are several faculty members from the university who live nearby, including several from the college that I serve as the academic dean. In the dailiness of my excursion back and forth between campus and home, I see few other Black folks. But more importantly to this story, the white folks who see me see very few other Black folks in their neighborhood.

One day, I was walking my dog – a pre-sister to Picklz, a 13-year-old Cocker Spaniel named PepperAnne, or Peppy for short – wearing my black hoodie and a knit cap. (Maybe I looked like Trayvon Martin.) We walked every morning and saw some of the same people: people walking their dogs and people leaving their homes in the morning to begin their days.

Peppy and I were a friendly duo, so we said good morning as we crossed paths with others during our morning ritual. Often, we paused as she, the dog, met and greeted her friends. It is an interesting thing to walk a dog, because I probably would not have much to talk about with many of these people, other than to exchange greetings. But the dogs seem to find a conversation of engagement that forces the humans to perform sociality.

On this morning, I saw a white woman who I had seen before walking her dog. I recognized her coming toward me from a distance on the sidewalk. She was slight of build, and her dog was bigger and maybe a little sturdier than Peppy.

The difference was that day, she continued moving in my direction as I moved in her direction; usually, she would cross the street before we encountered each other. (Dog walking etiquette is directional relative to driving a vehicle. Know your side of the street.) She was a person on whom the niceties of morning greetings were usually lost. While I would wave or say, "Good morning," or Peppy might bark, she would never respond. But this morning, she was walking toward me and not crossing. We got about 20 feet from each other and she began to scream, "Stay away from me! Stay away from me and my dog! I am warning you!"

She was really screaming! And at that point her dog became unruly, and she became entangled in his leash. I was not fully aware of what was going on in the moment, or whether the dog was in attack mode to protect his owner because of her screaming, or whether the attack mode is the true nature of the dog and she is trying to protect us (or herself). I only knew that she began to scream before the dog became unruly.

Because there are cars parked on the side of the road, my only option to avoid her was to walk into the yard next to me, and to walk the distance through the yard to pass the spectacle of which I was suddenly a part. Peppy led the way because she was scared, and she wanted to get away from both the barking dog and the screaming white woman.

In that moment, the screaming attracted the attention of other good white folks. Several of them paused, stood outside their cars, looked to see what was happening. I saw a few faces looking through windows of neighboring houses. The man whose yard I was crossing was now standing on his front porch with his hands on his hips.

It was a fucking 360-degree cinematic moment, with me at the center point, pivoting to see multiple pairs of white eyes staring at the scene, staring at me. In that moment, I was vulnerable to this historical legacy of relational dynamics: a white woman screaming in a white neighborhood at what appeared to be a Black man encroaching upon her, and other white people seemingly coming to her rescue.

> And I was one of their neighbors too.
>
> And I walked that path every morning.
>
> And I have a Ph.D. damn it!
>
> And I am an academic dean at the private Catholic (Jesuit) University that is a block away.
>
> But I am always Black man first, and none of the other traits offer me protection in that moment.

I offered the onlookers a befuddled look, as if to say,

> "I am confused too."
>
> "I don't know what is going on."

Or as if to say,

> "I am innocent."

But I said nothing and kept walking. And I didn't turn fully around but took only side glances to ensure that no one was following me. That morning, Peppy and I took an alternate route back home, and I never walked that stretch of road again.

The scene I have described could have been about the white woman warning me of her aggressive dog, or maybe there was mental illness involved, or maybe she was suffering from some socially experienced trauma (Note: I only include these speculations to appease the good white people in the audience/in this readership who demand that I give the white woman in the story the benefit of the doubt. Unlike the way I was treated and perceived in the story that I am telling, such consideration on my part as a Black man is a historical expectation for whiteness). There are missing pieces in her public performance that go unresolved.

> Like the actual evidence of threat, other than my Black male presence; or
>
> Like the specter of my snarling vicious cocker spaniel threatening an attack,
>
> Or even an apology.

Mary Weems reinforces: "You could have been killed or arrested."

I reflect on this story with some trepidation because of what could have been the consequence of that moment, both in the past and in the present. But here is another to drive home my point.

"Cover Her Up!"

This is a story is about another older white woman in the neighborhood.

That opening line could be a trope of the Black experience in America, because we all have stories about white women, older or younger, that test the limits of our humanity. But this is story about an older white woman who I would see every day in her bathrobe sweeping the sidewalk in front of her house. She never waived, and after several attempts, I stopped. Several times a week, I would see her Latina caregiver or housekeeper entering the house in the morning. She would wave. That particular morning, the morning of the happening, as I was passing with Peppy, I didn't see the older white woman sweeping the sidewalk, but I did see her Latina caregiver or housekeeper, waiving. But not just waiving; she was waiving me down. She was speaking frantically in broken English, asking for my help and leading me into the home.

I tied the dog's leash to the porch railings and entered the house. There, immediately to my right, in a front bedroom I saw the older white woman sprawled on the floor naked except for a thin night coat that was crumpled below her. Apparently, the older white woman had fallen onto the cold floor, and she couldn't get up – and her Latina care giver or housekeeper could not lift her alone. By the nature of my character, I needed to assist. The older white woman was crying on the floor. I couldn't tell if she was hurt or embarrassed, and it was obvious the presence of a Black man added alarm.

I turned away from the exposed body and told the Latina caregiver or housekeeper to cover her up. I would help but *cover her up* for her modesty or for my safety, which the Latina caregiver or housekeeper did. I approached the older white woman crying on the floor. Speaking in calming tones, I assured her that I only wanted to help her. After flinching several times at my touch through the added covering, she accepted my assistance. I placed her on the bed and exited the house quickly, not allowing time to receive appreciation from the Latina caregiver or housekeeper. I unleashed the dog and walked steadily but quickly away. Not running of course; a Black man running out of an older white woman's house would have drawn attention.

Later, on the phone, I told my older sister, who is a caregiver, what happened. And she immediately lashed into me, telling me to NEVER DO THAT AGAIN! She was not concerned that the older white woman on the floor could have been hurt, and maybe should not have been moved. She was reminding me that it was not just the older white woman who was vulnerable in that situation. The Latina caregiver or housekeeper was vulnerable. And I as, a Black man, was vulnerable to accusations of mistreating or attacking the vulnerability of a white woman. All she needed to do was cry "attack" and point the finger at me. All she needed was to scream: "Stay away from me! Stay away from me. I am warning you!" And my life would have been ended.

Mary Weems echoes my sister: NEVER DO THAT AGAIN! AND TRUST, I WON'T! Yet that is a lost piece of my human impulse that I mourn – a part of our humanness that has been taken from so many other Black folks. But there are countless other ways and instances to assist others that don't threaten our persons – and do not threaten the person that I am, and the person I want to be.

I reflect on this story with some trepidation because of what could have been the consequence of that moment, both in the past and in the present.

***

These last two stories pivot on the lingering effects of slavery and racism in America – particularly the relational history of white women and Black men. Here is a presumed vulnerable femininity versus a bestial masculinity, the Black penis as weapon and instrument of revenge to attack the purity of whiteness. Each encounter is a template for disaster grounded in issues of power and propriety, control and vulnerability in a fatal desire/disdain – a dynamic that helped sustain slavery and its legacy. This is also an iconic trope of Jim Crow laws relative to the Emmett Till case. Remember? A 14-year Black boy who was lynched in Mississippi in 1955, after being accused of flirting with – and thus offending – a 21-year-old white woman in her family's grocery store. The brutality of his murder by her white menfolk, and the fact that his killers were acquitted, drew attention to the long history of violent persecution of Black people in America. It further solidifies in modern times the legacy of slavery and the virtues of white women that must be defended.[6] Did I mention that he was a 14-year-old Black boy? What was the reparation to his family? The acquittal sent a message to all Black men about their roving eyes or hands on white women: not that desire is dangerous, and not that all white women or white people are dangerous, but that the escape clause is deadly.

Here I am interested in the difference between "payback" and "reparations." The savage murder of a 14-year-old Black boy as payback for his presumed disrespect of a 21-year-old white woman. The real narrative of what happened is not clear. I suspect that she found him cute, and she flirted and was caught by one of her white menfolk – and hence to save herself, she lied. That is also a historical narrative with similar outcomes; desire and disdain meet in an alchemy of violence and self-protection, using the prevailing laws of the land as escape.

Here, I am also interested in the rights given to white women to claim offense at Black boys and men. This right exists by virtue of a social system that prioritizes the claims, dignities, and lives of one party over the other. It represents a form of payback – or is it pay-it-forward – and the naturalized continuation of a demonic social propriety from slavery to the present. And to be honest, there are no reparations that can undue those histories, those moments, and those experiences had by many Black men and Black people in America, including the rape of thousands of Black women by white men throughout slavery and continuing to today.

> What reparations can be offered for the social disdain of blackness in America?
>
> What reparations can be offered for the racism and psychological stigma of blackness that has become part of the social framework in this country, even penetrating the psyche of some Blacks to believe their own devalued self-worth?
>
> What reparations can serve as payback for the lifetime of struggle of Black people in America?
>
> This is not an argument meant to forestall the efforts of reparations, but maybe added logics for the metrics used to measure the relevant harms.

There would be no reparations for me in either of the stories I've shared; with crying white women pointing fingers at me, the situations could have quickly turned tragic. And my life would have been gone. There is a historical legacy of legions of Black men who were outright killed, disappeared, or jailed after being accused by a white woman of something tragic, or even just something deemed inappropriate to their delicate sensibilities.

***

But I want to go back.

I want to go back to the young Black man who was driving the delivery truck. He was driving one of those blue steel-colored delivery trucks with the suggestive smile that also appears on every one of their packages, signifying care in delivery and satisfaction. I loved that encounter with this young Black brother. I felt that in that brief moment, he and I were, as ***Mary Weems writes: "spiritually vibing."*** Not just on the James Brown pronouncement of "The Payback," but we are two Black men finding an immediate connection through music, across age and life situations; bonded in blackness and the joys and the struggles of being Black in America. *Spiritual vibing* takes spiritual beliefs of God, nature, humanity, and/or cultural knowledge, and puts them into practice as recognition and a gesture of welcome to those with similar connections.[7] The music just added to the vibe, as a distinct emotional connective that drove the possibility of communion. Such is the case with collaborative spirit-writing.

I said to him:

"What do yoooou know about 'The Payback'"?

And we both laughed in that way that older Black men always kid younger Black boys as ritual play. And if it is delivered just right, they know you are teasing and trying to connect across generations. And he simply said,

"This is just good shit man. And I am waiting for mine."

And I simply said,
"O Yeah, Yeah you're right!"

As we waved and moved in opposite directions, still smiling and still bobbing our heads and singing, I thought: payback or reparations? I am sure that we have both given each some thought, as we listen to the continuing Black notes of our people.

Notes

1 Human Rights Watch. (2001, July 19). *An approach to reparations*. https://www.hrw.org/legacy/campaigns/race/reparations.htm.
2 Pitofsky, M. (2021). Police drop charges after Black teenager arrested while walking home amid winter storm. *The Hill*, 23 February. https://thehill.com/blogs/blog-briefing-room/news/540141-police-drop-charges-after-black-teenager-arrested-while-walking
3 This is an obvious reference to the Rev. Dr. Martin Luther King Jr's "I have a dream speech."
4 See: Simba, M. (2014). *The three-fifths clause of the United States Constitutions (1787)*. October 3. https://www.blackpast.org/african-american-history/events-african-american-history/three-fifths-clause-united-states-constitution-1787.
5 Alexander, B. K. (2017). Black male/white tower: A performative film auto-critography." In Gil Richard Musolf (Ed.), *Oppression and resistance: Structure, agency, transformation (TheBlue Ribbon Papers of Studies in Symbolic Interactionism)* (pp. 62–64). Emerald Publishing Limited.
6 See Emmett Louis Till. https://en.wikipedia.org/wiki/Emmett_Till.
7 Also see Spiritual Living Articles. https://www.theangelsmessages.com/blogs/spiritual-living/6-ways-to-spiritual-vibe-your-life.

20

SAY IT: OR REPARATIONS MY ASS?

Mary E. Weems

> *And to be honest, there are no reparations that can undo those histories, those moments, and those experiences had by many Black men and Black people in America, including the rape of thousands of Black women by white men throughout slavery and continuing to today.*
>
> – *Bryant Keith Alexander*

For me, this is the only difficult piece to write in our book. In the main because I've periodically thought long and hard about the issue of reparations for the descendants of former slaves in the United States. Yet, since I first became aware that there were Black folks working to secure various forms of compensation from a United States government founded by a Constitution which had to be amended to include us, I have never believed it had a snowball's chance in the desert of happening. This lack of belief in possibility has always been followed closely by what Bryant alludes to in the above quote: there is nothing that would come close to being enough.

When I read Bryant's "R-E-P-A-R-A-T-I-O-N-S" acrostic poem in "The Payback," which lays out the kinds of things Black people demand compensation for, it was so comprehensive, I had nothing to add. Yet, it did make me think about the fact that it would have been horrible enough for slaves to endure the atrocities of slavery even if they had then been let go after the Civil War and been allowed to freely pursue a successful life with all of the rights and privileges afforded to white citizens of the United States.

BUT no!

Thanks to race hatred and a fundamental belief by the majority – we've always had white supporters, even during slavery – that we are inferior, coupled with an unwillingness to risk sharing even a modicum of power, following a brief

DOI: 10.4324/9781003203520-20

Reconstruction period, white men immediately put laws, practices, and policies, both formal and informal in place, to make certain that a racist, oppressive foundation was woven into all of this country's major institutions. The spheres of education, employment, housing, judicial, and local, state, federal government were all designed to limit, as much as possible, any opportunity for Black people to succeed in pursing the American Dream promised to all who immigrated here for a better life.

It is March 2, 2021, and Black people are still regularly being harassed by police, shot and killed by police. Black men can't walk, jog, bird watch, stand still, breathe, or exist without risking their lives and/or freedom. Black women, along with our Black men and children, are constantly stereotyped in all forms of social and mass media – including television programming, commercials, magazines, and various live streaming programs – as being inferior to our white counterparts. When we own property, it is more likely to be appraised at less than its actual market value. When we are hired, unless the hourly pay or salaries are public knowledge, we're more likely to be paid less than our white counterparts. We comprise the overwhelming majority of people filling the prisons (both men and women), and a majority of people (disproportionately) dying from the COVID-19 virus. In terms of assets, according to the 2019 Survey of Consumer Finances (SCF) posted on the Board of Governors of the Federal Reserve System, our current collective net worth is eight times lower than the typical white family. The SCF defines wealth as "the difference between a families' gross assets and their liabilities":[1]

Race/Ethnicity	Median (Typical)	Mean (Average)
Whites	$188,200	983,400
Blacks	**$24,100**	142,500
Hispanics	$36,100	165,500

Meaning that 401 years after the first slaves were brought here in 1619 and 165 years after the legal ending of slavery, Black descendants of slaves – who did not choose to immigrate here for a better life – and Black people who contributed free labor to the foundation of wealth in this country for white people in general, and for several businesses and major corporations in particular, through Convict Leasing, remain on the bottom of the bottom when compared to all major race/ethnic groups included in the data collection.

As I was taking notes for this piece, last night, I watched a news clip on YouTube of George Takei, Japanese activist, star of the original Star Trek, and World War II Internment Camp survivor. Takei talked about the increase in hate crimes against Asian Americans during and since the Trump era, thanks in part to Trump repeatedly blaming China for the coronavirus. As I watched, I recalled that Japanese Americans, inspired by the Civil Rights Movement, fought for reparations for years and had finally received them. A quick Google search revealed that President Ronald Reagan finally signed the Civil Liberties Act in 1988 to compensate Japanese Americans for their unjust internment during World War II, when many lost their businesses and/or everything they owned and were held in inhumane conditions until the end of the war. That compensation included two things: 1) A formal apology, and 2) $20,000 to each surviving victim.[2]

Considering the cultural shame inflicted on interred Japanese Americans – while in many cases their relatives were simultaneously risking their lives in various branches of the military – and given the generational economic loss, an apology and $20,000 per person seems like an almost insignificant compensation. But as I continued to read, I discovered the reasoning behind accepting these inadequate sums. Tateishi, the leader of the Japanese Reparations Movement, stated: "There is a saying in Japanese culture, *kodomo no tante ni,* which means 'for the sake of the children,' and for us running the campaign this had much to do with it. [...] It's the legacy we're handing down to them, and to the nation, to say that, 'You can make this mistake, but you also have to correct it – and by correcting it, hopefully not repeat it again."

By referencing Japanese children and the importance of letting them know that when someone treats you unjustly, you should not let them get away with it, I'm left with a new way of considering whether Black people should follow the example of Japanese Americans and continue to seek even minimal reparations. This is why I changed the titled of this writing by ending with a question mark, rather than with my original exclamation point.

As has happened many times during our spirit-writing journey to create this book, Bryant and I have been on the same page without knowing it. Just as he borrowed from James Brown's music for "The Payback," I'd already decided to include my poem "Say It" to honor Brown's memory, his revolutionary music, and its direct influence on my life.

My family on both sides migrated from either North or South Carolina at the beginning of the 20th century. My great-grandparents on both sides had been long dead by the time I was born. I'm from a poor working class, single-parent, northern background, during a time when children were supposed to be seen and not heard. This means the adults in our family used to send us out of the room when they wanted to share stories about living in a racist America, and I can recall only rare occasions when I had the opportunity to overhear all or part of a story – mainly because I was nosey and would sometimes hide close by and listen.

But I grew up during the 1960s. As a result, thanks to televised news reports of Black people being attacked by dogs, beat down by police and arrested (like now) for peaceful, non-violent protesting: being an avid reader: my own experiences then and now; and the shared stories of siblings, cousins, and other younger family members, I grew up with a clear understanding of just how racist this country was and is.

A pivotal moment in my young life, in terms of identity, occurred during a time when a Black person could get into a fight for calling someone Black, which at the time was meant as an insult. Then, just 4 months after Dr. Martin Luther King was Assassinated, James Brown came out with "Say it Loud (I'm Black and I'm Proud)," in August of 1968. Almost overnight, being Black and proud was in, and dashikis, afros, Black hair care products, plastic afro picks with fists at the end of them, and raised right fists indicating "Black Power" became popular, as did more Black people organizing to work together for our greater good. James Brown and his music affected an entire generation at just the right moment, and I will forever be grateful to him for it.

The following poem was inspired by Brown's song. Recently, reading several poems by young, Black poets from poor, working class backgrounds, I realized that many of the themes they're writing about now are things I was living and writing about when I was their age.

Say It.

For: James Brown

Five forever's of reading poems

and I

can still

t-r-a-c-e our story in lines________________________________

of Black poets

I'll never meet:

Heating the house

with the oven

boiling water for dishes

and washing up – salad

dressing sandwiches

tricking McDonald's

for food.

Know

I've had enough for years but still

recall how to stretch

a passed down shoe

save bus fare for candy by walking every other day
Every time lights and gas stop working I think:
"Did I pay the bill?"
When I/cut/myself
in the/kitchen/I use
peroxide and a band-aide never
realizing until I see the scar
that I should have gone
to hospital I fear almost as much as …
If I could come back as an animal
it would be a stray dog kind
that used to run my neighbor
hood/dare a rat/to cross its path/
a cat to *meow*
tough as the black dirt
in our front yard
they never bit or bothered us
unlike the well-trained dogs
I'm around now
whose owners pick up their shit
buy them fancy coats and hats
let the dogs walk them.
Poor/Proud/People
could be my epitaph
alliteration to Blackness
until.

Nowadays, when I hear Black folks complain about young Black men – including my husband – who wear their pants sagging so low you can see their entire underwear-covered asses, I'm reminded of when our slave asses/bodies were the number one asset of white men. I remember that we are still struggling for some of the same justice we've been fighting for, for centuries, and it makes me smile to think that just maybe these young men are metaphorically telling racist white folks to kiss their ass.

Notes

1 Federal Reserve. (2020). *Survey of consumer finances.* https://www.federalreserve.gov/econres/scfindex.htm.
2 Qureshi, B. (2013, August 9). From wrong to right: A U.S. apology for Japanese internment. *NPR.* https://www.npr.org/sections/codeswitch/2013/08/09/210138278/japanese-internment-redress?t=1618781881237.

SECTION V
Introduction to Redemption

Bryant Keith Alexander and Mary E. Weems

On the notion of "redemption," **Mary Weems states**:

> "Like most word definitions, they vary a bit based on where you look. When I looked up the word Redemption in my Oxford English Dictionary, 1996 edition, 'Redemption' was defined *Redemption (n) 1. Redeeming or being redeemed 2. Thing that redeems.* But when I looked up 'Redeem,' there were eleven (11) different definitions. Here are the ones which resonated with me in our section: 3. *Convert into goods or cash* **(like selling slaves for money?)** 4. *Deliver from sin and damnation* **(like white folks justified slavery by using 'manifest destiny' or the belief that they'd been ordained by God to save the lowly Black folk?)** 8. *Purchase the freedom of a person* **(something that white folks did for slaves not-enough?).** Most importantly, I noticed that the origin of the word *redeem* is from the Latin *emo* which means to 'buy.'"

I agree with Mary. Definitions vary a bit based on where you look, but I would also suggest that they vary by how you are looking, who is looking, and why they are looking. Sometimes, we look for definitions to inform and educate ourselves about what we don't know. Sometimes, we look for definitions to find words to articulate the felt sensations of the spirit. And sometimes, we look for definitions to confirm what we already know, in an activism of truth-finding and truth-making.

The notion of redemption for us – and not just in this section, but how it plays throughout this book – is tied up in a desire for Black folks in America to be recognized in the depth of our humanity and to receive the fullness of our denied rights, privileges, and freedoms. Ours is a desire to be released from the shackles of this world, though not through death. The cornerstone of many religious

DOI: 10.4324/9781003203520-105

ideologies is a form of salvation that involves the changing of shapes and forms to enter the grace of *Beulah land* (look that one up). But, we are not talking about that ultimate redemption from the physical world. We want redemption in our living now – not in our dying have lived.

We offer new definitions:

1. **Redemption** is the shifting and fusing of the political and cultural lens of our social perception. 2. **Redemption** is a reunification of our mind, body, and spirit which slavery brutally severed. 3. **Redemption** is not just a thing done, but a thing doing, an active process of resolve. 4. **Redemption** is a reidentification with our cultural cosmologies before we were stripped, bought, and sold – and resold, and resold, and sold out, and renamed. 5. **Redemption** is when we change the refrain of our life song to something with continual uplift and possibility: a new song. 6. **Redemption** is a shift to complete PRIDE in our being, which is not just for Black people, but all Black, Indigenous, People of Color, and our interlocking and intersectional struggles with our Lesbian, Gay, Bisexual, Transgender, Intersex, Queer, Curious, Asexual, Pansexual, Gender-non-conforming, Gender-Fluid, Non-binary, and Androgynous+ colleagues as selves, in a struggle to claim our empowered voices and spaces in a new world of possibilities. As our sister Audre Lorde wrote, we are engaged in a "Litany of Survival."[1] And while it may be "better to speak remembering we were never meant to survive," we do survive! And we have and will continue to survive! 7. **Redemption** is not only that which is done to us, or for us, by an enlightened society or by individual divine saviors. 8. **Redemption** is also what we do for ourselves: how we RE- Member ourselves into our destined possibilities of being.

21

BLACK NOTES

Bryant Keith Alexander

I have been thinking a lot about "Black notes."

In a powerful solo performance entitled "BLACKNOTES," Mary E. Weems explains: "Original Negro Spirituals were composed of only the Black keys on a piano. Some say it was the sounds that come from the bowels of slave ships. Like the Sankofa bird, which in the Akan language of Ghana means 'to reach back and get it,' … [my] 'Black Notes' begins by returning to the past, then moving forward through contemporary moments both lived and imagined." The performance uses "auto/ethnography, poetic, and narrative inquiry to investigate the Black experience through a cultural lens which shifts from the personal to the political."

Auto/ethnography – especially when constructed with the separating and connecting slash – signifies the simultaneity of being both exclusive and inclusive, *a present and continuous* relationality of the individual to culture: a collaborative relationality that is both personal and political. And in this case, one Black body stands in relation to a history of Black bodies giving voice to truth, channeling and unshackling bodies, memories, and voices through performance and performative writing. The performance is poignant for many reasons, but mostly because of its beautiful and complicated simplicity. Choreographic movements that show the Black body in motion, in locomotion. The Black body is anchored in place by a spread of kente cloth on the floor and pivots in a practiced way to African-American experiences in the United States, with Africa at the root center of a worldview. The performance is a sole Black voice telling universal stories of Black experience. The poetic and narrative voice are Black notes to, of, and about Black people.

DOI: 10.4324/9781003203520-21

In the performance, the use of familiar Negro spirituals like "Sometime I Feel like a Motherless Child" and "Amazing Grace" speak to spiritual strivings: a longing for the idea of mother/land and salvation – both a return and a departure – that we all share. A strong, Black female body on the stage speaks across the experience of many, and the unorchestrated yet expected sound of groans, shouts, laughter, and maybe crying come from an audience drawn into both the performance and the shared history it narrates. Hence, the performance is *a call and response*, a collaborative spirit meaning-making that transcends the performance as entertainment to become more like a townhall, church meeting, or revival – in which Black folks attend to business through the spirit.

I have been thinking a lot about "Black notes."

Black notes scribbled on the walls of "The Door of No Return" in the African slave trade leading across the middle passage; messages written in words, scratches, tears, shit, piss, and wails that trigger and reverberate the Black notes of our existence. Like the Shroud of Turin, Black notes leave a negative image of the scourged and crucified history of our people. The imprint is produced by the alchemy of (white) man's inhumanity to (Black) wo/man, a biochemical residue from body oils and intense spiritual energy activated on the tapestry of our lives to create the ghosting image of African slave bodies in the bowels of ships, seamlessly pressed against each other and against the wooden surfaces of their captivity, melding, and melting on the chains of their restraint. The lashing belts and whips to their backs create a dirge of pain, and *the tracks of their tears* (think Smokey Robinson)[2]:

> Refrain of the lash followed by the verse of pain.
>
> Refrain of the lash followed by the verse of pain.
>
> Refrain of the lash followed by the verse of pain, with a haunting musicality.

All striking a chord of inhumanity pressed against the will to survive. These are documentations, remembrances, and reminders; tortured discordant Black notes that resonate dissonance over distance, echoing over time to the present – like the cries of our brother Eric Garner:

> "I Can't Breathe!"
>
> "I Can't Breathe!"
>
> "I Can't Breathe!"

"I Can't Breathe!"

"I Can't Breathe!"

"I Can't Breathe!"

"I Can't Breathe!"

"I Can't Breathe!"

"I Can't Breathe!"

"I Can't Breathe!"

Eleven **times** before losing consciousness and **dying** – murdered.[3]

I have been thinking a lot about "Black notes."

Dancing Black notes on a social grid with a lot of white space.

I am thinking about "Black Note," the Black American jazz ensemble, and so many other Black ensembles remembered by people of a certain age, like *The Temptations, Earth Wind and Fire, The Isley Brothers, The Whispers, The Jackson Five (not just the Jacksons), The Four Tops, The Chi-Lites, The Supremes, Parliament–Funkadelic, The Staple Singers, Gladys Knight and the Pips, Booker T. and the M.G.'s,* just to name a few. These artists were coordinated and choreographed Black notes that embodied and promoted the culture with style and grace, but not without having to traverse the borderlines of race that penetrated every aspect of their musical journeys as Black people in America. Yet, they persisted as storytellers of the Black experience through Black notes and expressive arts.

And I am also thinking about those Black gospel voices that twisted and trailed Black notes with vocal trills, tremolos, and trivolettes that twist and turn, their notes sustained with natural vibratos. People like *Mahalia Jackson, Sissy Houston, The Mighty Clouds of Joy, The Dixie Hummingbirds,* the original *Five Blind Boys of Alabama, The Clark Sisters,* and don't forget *Ri Ri – Aretha Franklin* – all *holding God in their throat.* The Black notes that came through their voices were supported by diaphragmatic breathing, but actually emanated from their souls; from *the souls of Black folks* (think W.E.B. Du Bois).[4]

I have been thinking about the power in Black musical traditions, trumpeting, and wailing tones from *voices as instruments* and *instruments as voices*, amplifying the Black experience in this country. In spirituals, jazz, blues, hip hop, rhythm and blues, rap, and reggae (giving birth to reggaeton), sounds and words and expressions make the soul leap, the spirit weep, and the body sway. We sway in such a way that the polyrhythms of our ancestral bodies illustrate a communicative musicality that is ancient, flowing from rich places beyond the cognitive and deep within the blood lines that we can trace back – back to the places from which we were snatched.

I see the movement and sway whether in a Masai welcome dance in Kenya, Africa, or at the Black night clubs in the South. Earth-centered dancing, rhythmic and percussive, unstifled in fluidity, with bounce that catches the notes in the air and brings the beats back to the ground. Working between the beats with body parts absorbing notes and rhythms as they flow in sound, dangling and shifting body parts making new notes to be felt, seen, and heard. Adding to the music, making music leap and live: music and dance as embodied cultural performances. Blood and bodies remember.

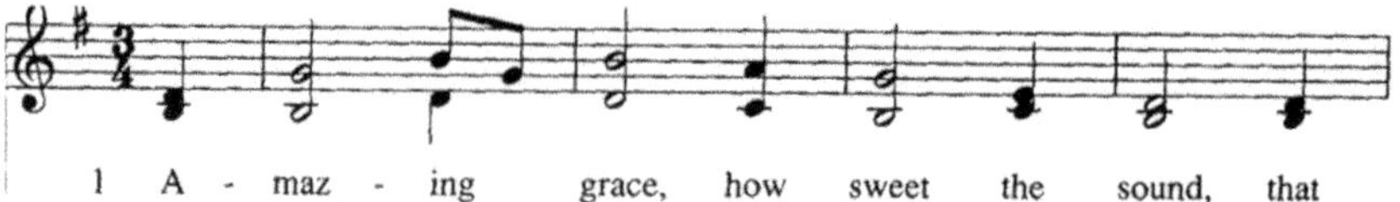

I have been thinking a lot about "Black notes" in the collaborative spirit-writing with our ancestors, and between Mary and me in our particularity and plurality.

I have been thinking about the ways in which Black notes are necessarily different from white notes in collaborative autoethnography; one is necessarily seen, and sometimes considered conspicuous, under surveillance, behind bars, hanging on bars, and considered unruly.

In musical terms:

fortississimo	*fff* very very loud
fortissimo	*ff* very loud
forte	*f* Loud

Black notes, as related to Black people, are sometime considered loud, very loud, too loud; and hence uncivil to the Western or European canon – even when we are crying for help in everyday life through our music.

Not to be reductive, but the opposite of Black notes is *white noise*: "a colloquialism to describe a backdrop of ambient sound, creating an indistinct commotion, seamless [such that] no specific sounds composing it as a continuum can be isolated as a veritable instance of some familiar sound."[5] White noise is the persistent promotion of white privilege that dominates the cultural landscape. It's a performative that, even in the preponderance of its existence, enacts and erases the nature of itself, becoming an unsound – but not silence.

White noise is so common and every day in the lives of Black people that it both fades as a repetition of the same line of a staid musical trope with no meaning, or it lingers in the memory as a caution or a curious nonsense. It is like elevator music that you hate, but yet you find yourself humming it all day, until you just have to either shoot yourself or put on some church music – or some *Sly and Family Stones* – to get some real funk of your own-making back into your head. To get you on the right track of your own blackness – not the version of blackness that is nullified in white noise.

I have been thinking a lot about Black notes like love letters to Black people. These are the notes written in secret code that only Black people can read, like notes slipped into the school lockers of secret crushes or passed around to announce the secret meeting behind the barn at midnight. But also, they're the loud stereophonic Black notes that you deliver in the music blasting out of your car, making white folks turn their heads – but making other Black folks say, "Yeah, you're right!" They're the Black notes that you still play from your vinyl records – albums and 45s, maybe even 8-track tapes – when Black people come over to your crib, because the quality of sound seems more authentic and the labor of love more palpable. The sheer fact is that the modality of the message expresses the meaning of the moment. You write love letters kneeling on one knee at protest marches or raising a fist in the air at an athletic game or wearing your favorite **Black Lives Matter** t-shirt to your white workplace (or in the background of your ZOOM room) to make a point. Black-notes-as-love-letters sing both mournfully and hopefully. They say, "I see my blackness. I see your blackness." And then they give you, your brothers, and your sisters (and those who live in between) the authority to join with James Brown and sing, *"Say It Loud – I'm Black and I'm Proud"* – without apology.[6]

Throughout this piece, I have been thinking about God's "Amazing Grace" and the gift of that grace through which we were once lost and now found – and the collaborative spirit that has been essential to our survival.

Black notes from our ancestors read: "Don't forget. We are with you always. We are in you, always." Soul strong and spirit proud.

Notes

1 Lorde, A (1978.) *The black unicorn* (pp. 31–32). W.W. Norton and Company.
2 Robinson, S. & The Miracles. (n.d.). The tracks of my tears. *Lyrics*. https://www.lyrics.com/lyric/32568739/Smokey+Robinson+%26+the+Miracles/The+Tracks+of+My+Tears.

3 Eric Garner died 17 July 2014 in a police chokehold. See History.com Editors. (n.d.). Eric Garner dies in NYPD Chokehold. *History.com*. https://www.history.com/this-day-in-history/eric-garner-dies-nypd-chokehold.
4 DuBois, W.E.B. (1903). *The souls of black folk*. A.C. McClurg & Co.
5 *White noise (slang)*. (2019, June 4.) *Wikipedia*. https://en.wikipedia.org/wiki/White_noise.
6 Brown, J. (n.d.). Say It Loud (I'm black and I'm proud). *Lyrics*. https://www.lyrics.com/lyric/12634/James+Brown/Say+It+Loud+%28I%27m+Black+and+I%27m+Proud%29.

22

BLACK, BLACK NOTES – 2-24-2021

Mary E. Weems

Me and Bryant began collaborating in-spirit when he brought me in to perform my one-woman "Black Notes" at Loyola Marymount University on February 18, 2016.

Bryant Keith Alexander gets me. We connect, our spirits, conjoining, ebbing, and flowing like the Nile River – the kind of in-spirit collaborative connection you can't construct, contrive, or make up. You can't plan it, wish for it, dream about it. If it is going to happen, it does, and while I've collaborated at some level over the years with other folks, ours is a once-in-a-lifetime pairing, one I know I won't have again with anyone else.

When I read his new piece "Black Notes," inspired by my performance text/play about the Black experience, I immediately wrote him to share how much I love it. We have a rhythm of engagement in writing – to the point that this current book project is already being written even as our previous effort is "in-press."

Then, as I was returning home from a dentist's appointment this afternoon, some of the lines in the work grabbed me. As I soon as I got home, I printed the piece off, grabbed a yellow highlighter, and started spiritually vibing on lines I divided in to separate sections, one per page, resulting in a textual quintet. The only lines I added to this "found poem" were the lines of song for Mahalia Jackson and Aretha Franklin.[1] And to make the sections of the quintet fit, I occasionally altered words – for example, from "laughing" to "laughs."

I titled this piece "Black, black Notes" because the first "Black" represents Black people, and the second "black" represents musical notes:

I.

I have been thinking about "Black Notes"

DOI: 10.4324/9781003203520-22

Negro Spirituals
Black keys on a piano
Slave ships.
One Black body a history of Black bodies motion
in locomotion
place a spread of kente cloth African experiencesssssssss
the root center of world
Black telling stories of Black
Black notes *Motherless Chile Grace* a longing for return
and departure
Black female body speaking un-orchestrated groans shouts
Laughs
Cries
com-inggggggggg
through the spirit.

II.

I have been thinking about "Black Notes"
Scribbled on the walls of The Door in the African slave trade
Messages written scratches, tears, shit, piss, crucified history
Produced by the (white) man residue from body oils
intense spiritual energy tapestry African slave bodies
pressed against each
wooden surfaces
chains, lashing belts, backs, pain, *the track of their tears*
(thank you Smokey Robinson)
Refrain pain
Refrain verse
Refrain lash

the will to survive

Remembrances and Reminders Black notes dissonance

Echoing Eric Garner:

"I can't Breathe!

I

Can't

I Can't

I Can't

I Can't

Bre

athe!!!!!!!!!!!

Dying"

III.

I am thinking "Black Notes"

Black American jazz

remembered

people age

like *The Temptations*

coordinated and choreographed

Black notes embodied and promoted culture

with style and grace

borderlines of race

musical journeys in America

Storytellers Black notes

expressive arts

Black Gospel twisted Black notes

trills, tremolos and trivolettes

sustained notes

Mahalia Jackson *"Precious Lord, take my hand, lead me on*
let me stand"
Aretha Franklin "*when my soul was in the lost and found"*
you came along to claim it"
hold God in their throats
their voices breathing from the souls
of Black folks.
Spirituals, jazz, blues, hip hop, rhythm and blues, rap, reggae
Expressions that make the soul weep
Body sway ancient rich blood lines
We can trace to the places we were snatched.
welcome dance in the South
catch the notes in the air
bring beats back to the ground
body parts notes rhythms
dangling new notes felt
Blood and bodies remember.

IV.

I have been thinking "Black notes"
Black notes different from white notes
in collaborative auto/ethnography
one is seen
considered conspicuous
under surveillance
behind bars hanging
and unruly musical
uncivil to Europeans
even crying everyday

through our music
the opposite of Black notes is *white noise*
a backdrop of ambient sound
indistinct commotion
a continuum
persistent promotion of white privilege
erases the nature of itself
becoming an unsound
sssssssssssssssssssssssssssssssssssilence
White noise is so common in the lives of Black people it fades
with no meaning lingers
a curious non-sense like elevator music you hate
but hum until you have to either shoot yourself
or put on some real funk
getting you on the right track of your own
Blackness.

V.

I have been thinking about Black
Love letters to Black people
notes written in secret code only Black people can read
notes that you slip in the school locker of your secret crush notes
you secretly pass around
announcing the meeting behind the barn at midnight.
Loud stereophonic Black notes in the music blasting out of your car
that makes white folks turn
but makes other Black folks say "Yeah!"
Black notes you play from vinyl records albums and 45s
when Black people come to your crib

authentic labors of love

the message the meaning of the moment

Love letters like kneeling at protest marches

raising a fist

wearing your favorite **Black Lives Matter** t-shirt to your white workplace

Black notes that sing – h-o-p-e

Black notes that say I see your Blackness

Brothers and sisters

Say it Loud – I'm Black and I'm Proud

Without

apology.

Note

1 *Precious lord, natural woman.* Mahalia Jason (1956) on the album "Bless this House" (Columbia Records CL 899); Aretha Franklin (1967). "(You Make Me Feel Like) A Natural Woman." single. Atlantic Records.

23

TAIL END AND SPIRITS-FREE

Bryant Keith Alexander

At the tail end of this project, I was waiting for Mary to respond to the finalizing statement for this book contract. I waited. Then there was an email from her that took my breath away:

***

From: Mary Weems <maryeweems45@gmail.com>

Sent: Friday, March 5, 2021 3:54 AM

To: Alexander, Bryant Keith <bryantkeithalexander@lmu.edu>

Subject: Yesterday would have been Michelle's 38th birthday

I spent the day remembering and reflecting. Sorry, I didn't get back to Hannah then, because she's off today.

Enjoy your weekend.

Mary

***

My heart sank because I also remembered, nearly four years prior, the email still sitting in a folder to be reviewed and remembered, when she wrote:

***

From: mary weems <maryeweems45@gmail.com>

Date: Monday, December 18, 2017 at 5:25 AM

DOI: 10.4324/9781003203520-23

To: “Alexander, Bryant Keith” <bryantkeithalexander@lmu.edu>

Subject: Miami beach & You

Sitting on balcony in Miami enjoying the ocean courtesy of sista-Friend Carien who wanted to spend time helping me heal. We went to UIUC together and she loved Michelle…

Thinking of you, feeling blessed that we’ve connected brother.

Happy holidays to you and your partner. See you next year.

love,

Mary

***

I wrote back in stilted stanza that no man can fully understand of a woman, a Black woman/mother, who has just lost her only child. But I tried to engage her heart, as I tried to engage her previous words on the subject of her loss, in a way in which our collaborative spirit-writing, even at that early stage, would allow. I wrote:

***

On December 18, 2017 11:27 AM, “Alexander, Bryant Keith” <bryant-keithalexander@lmu.edu> wrote:

Dearest Mary,

There is a lovely image in my head of you near the ocean…

Gathering memories of your daughter

like seashells on the shore that return from the depths of the ocean,

longing to be discovered

Infant toss in air—
now forever floating
in heart, in air, in memory
She is like the waves,
gently caressing the shore,
foam tickling the toes of memory
She is in the foam
In the breeze
In the faint smell of the ocean
Like the *smell of baby feet* that lingers

Not in the nose but in the heart of memory
She is the wave gently caressing the shore
tempting to return but always retreating,
on the other end of the cord again
forever gone and forever connected at the same time.
Best, Bryant

***

And with a free spirit, she wrote back:

***

From: mary weems <maryeweems45@gmail.com>

Sent: Monday, December 18, 2017 11:12 AM

To: Alexander, Bryant Keith <bryantkeithalexander@lmu.edu>

Subject: Re: Miami beach & You

Crying…will have this forever. W send pic soon. Love u…

***

Collaborative spirit-writing takes on many forms. In this closing section of the book, entitled *Redemption,* I turn back and bend time. I recall and remember this exchange with my sista-friend with sentiments of care that will recur for her like a pained and joyous anniversary, overlapping at the intersections of birth and death, as a reminder and remembrance over a lifetime. In the alliteration of our current exploration—in revolution, resistance, reimagining, reparations, and redemption—we are reminded of our connections to each other.

The body remembers,

birth and loss,

and the pained and inherited memories of our ancestors,

of our brothers and sisters suffering both near and far,

then and now,

on the streets driving/walking while Black,

in their homes with *a crack in the door.*

and deep within the middle passages of our past and future,

where we live now.

The body remembers,

like the scars we bare on our own skin,

trails of pain that we wear with shame,

trails of pain that we bear with pride, because we survive.

Spirit-work connects us to the living and the memory of those who have passed—forcing a reckoning of history and a confrontation of current realities. How do we work together? Working to remember, heal, and act toward promises yet to be fulfilled? How do we work collaboratively in and with our spirits?

My sista Mary has the last words of this book

Bryant Keith Alexander

24

3-4-2021 EARLY A.M. DREAM

Mary E. Weems

> *I'm in my car. It's winter, and Ice-T is in the front seat beside me. We are talking about the weather, and I look down and notice snow on the floor, just inside the driver's side door, which for some reason is cracked. I feel Michelle in the back seat. Next, we are on the street. I'm riding a bike (something I've only done on the street "once" in my adult life, when I was 21, in New York City of all places), and Michelle and Ice-T are walking behind me. Michelle never says a word, and I don't see her, but I know she's there. I share a concern about being late for a meeting, yet a few seconds later stop my bike to say that there's a bar ahead. "We could stop for a drink since Michelle is of age." I wake up.*

I've dreamt about Michelle four times since her suicide on January 3, 2017. Each of the first three times, I could clearly see my sweetie-pie, her same-color-as-me face, her dark black hair topped off with a widow's peak, her beautiful, unique, confident, independent-as-hell self. This dream, on what would have been her 38th birthday is the first time I didn't see her physically, but felt her spirit, our connection as strong as the umbilical cord that used to hold us together.

Message to Mama

Mama hold my hand and don't let

go, mama hold my hand and don't let go

even after I've learned to love *me* on my own,

mama don't let go not even if I'm grown. As I rest in

the room of your womb watching the way you look and walk,

DOI: 10.4324/9781003203520-24

> listening to you talk to me, sing to me, hold me with both hands
> like a gift – I remember the last time I was here, a hundred years ago
> growing in my last mama's room, smaller than this, and no kisses at
> night I remember the life I lived, short, to the point with no chance to
> be all I was to be – the last time a boy, never to know the joy of giving a
> chance at life. When I left I told God I wanted to come back a girl, a girl
> in you, seeing you growing up, falling in love then falling in love with me
> once you knew I was here, and your hands, brown as bread, brown as the
> last tree, your hands, always making a way to make a better way for you
> and your first child your hands, rubbing the place where you and I come
> together letting me know that all the warmth doesn't come from the sun
> your hands, that will touch me for the first time, just in time for giving
> thanks, your hands that will hold mine, and mold mine and comfort
> mine across this street some call life. Mama don't let go, never,
> ever let go, hold me mama, hold me.

I felt so blessed when I woke up and realized she'd come to see me, to let me know her spirit had moved a bit closer to God, that she'd be waiting to come back to get me when it's time.

I raised my daughter to believe in God, to always take time to pay attention to the gift God provides in nature. We used to watch the sky's infinitely changing landscape together, the sunrises and sunsets, the clouds before rainstorms. When she was little, she once told my babysitter "It's cold outside because God has the window to the sky open." We loved to walk together by the water. Something about it brought us even closer together, and I remember the first time I taught her how to skip a rock.

Water is the liquid of life. It's what protects a baby in the womb, it's where the spirits of too many of our slave ancestors rest whispering their stories. It gives me comfort to know that my daughter is with my familial ancestors, wrapped in the loving arms of my grandmother and grandfather, granny's eight sisters and three brothers and so many others – A spiritual reunion.

My brotha Bryant's poem reflects an ability we share: to empathize with others, doing our best to get closer to what they're experiencing to help them heal, to help ourselves heal, by letting them know we care. This book has been a labor of love by two people who are Black and woke, and embrace what it means to celebrate Blackness, in the midst of everyday struggle. Enjoy – in the spirit.

Milton Keynes UK
Ingram Content Group UK Ltd.
UKHW050044180724
445610UK00008B/44